D1714450

Freud's Dora

Freud's Dora

A Psychoanalytic, Historical, and Textual Study

Patrick J. Mahony

Yale University Press   New Haven and London

Designed by James J. Johnson and
set in Meridien type by Keystone Typesetting, Inc., Orwigsburg, Penn.
Printed in the United States of America by BookCrafters, Inc., Chelsea, Mich.

Library of Congress Cataloging-in-Publication Data

Mahony, Patrick, 1932–
    Freud's Dora : a psychoanalytic, historical, and textual study /
Patrick J. Mahony.
    p. cm.
    Includes bibliographical references and index.
    ISBN 0-300-06622-8 (alk. paper)

    1. Hysteria—Case studies.   2. Psychoanalysis—Case studies.
3. Bauer, Ida, 1882–1945—Mental health.   4. Freud, Sigmund,
1856–1939.   I. Title.
RC532.M34   1996
616.85′2409—dc20   96-10372

A catalogue record for this book is available from the British Library.

The paper in this book meets the guidelines for permanence and durability of
the Committee on Production Guidelines for Book Longevity of the Council on
Library Resources.

2   4   6   8   10   9   7   5   3   1

To Pierrette, our children, and the preciously near,
becoming ever more precious

Cowardice puts on prudence as a ready mask.
Courage simply is—and does not like being worn.

Contents

Preface

Nowadays the clinical vignette is popular in psychoanalytic literature, yet it cannot match the case history in longitudinal scope.
The dearth of published case histories is not surprising, however.
The many reasons include the synthetic challenge posed by the
wealth of data flooding any analysis; the multiple psychodynamic
complexities in every patient's life, whose explanation is complicated in turn by divergent theories found in the ever-increasing
mass of secondary literature; and the compositional obstacles to
writing any effective case history. I shall make a further claim. Of
all psychoanalytic genres, the case history is the most difficult
both to write and to read. Sadly, the complexity of these activities
eludes the awareness of most analysts, their training being
skewed toward how to listen and speak. Such a communicative
disparity in the formation of analysts has contributed to the current crisis besetting psychoanalysis and to its lack of credibility in
the academic marketplace.

The chronological entanglements peculiar to the case history
can be baffling. The order of experiences in the patient's life and
their delayed impact can be jumbled in the processes of remembering, understanding, and forgetting and presented with yet a
different ordering when the patient conveys them in analysis. All
these mental activities and experiences weave into the history of
the patient's transferential relationship with the analyst. The intri-
cate unfolding of the transference interacts with the analyst's

understanding, suppression, and repression of the patient's material. The analyst's communication of her or his understanding and misunderstanding possesses an order of its own; and finally, a new narrative order is found in the case history. To Freud's credit, he told Carl Jung that one can only describe a case history, not narrate it. A feature distinguishing Freud's case histories from others is that they contain repeated avowals about the very impossibility of writing an adequate case history.

Empathy poses a timely problem of its own in the composition of a case history. More than ever before, analysts speak about the clinical impact of empathy that is based on a transitory identification with the patient. Yet the absence of internalizability characterizes much of psychoanalytic prose today. To say this in somewhat different words, insofar as much writing in contemporary psychoanalytic journals and books is insipid, it tends to be noninternalizable. The medium undercuts the message when impersonal prose is used to advocate empathy, when noninternalizable prose is used to promote internalization.

Glossing the current psychoanalytic debate over internalizability, we may cite Ernest Jones (1955, 2:274) as he addresses Freud's case histories:

> The case history known as that of the "Wolfman" is assuredly the best of the series. Freud was then at the very height of his powers, a confident master of his method, and the technique he displays in the interpretation and synthesis of the incredibly complex material must win every reader's admiration. Only those who have tried can appreciate how difficult it is to present a long analysis in a coherent and interesting fashion. Few other analysts have succeeded in holding their readers' attention for more than the first pages. Here Freud's unusual literary powers and his capacity for coordinating masses of facts made him easily supreme.

We can carry on Jones's thought by saying that case writers must be judged for the empathic contact that they express not only with the patient but also with the reader—no mean chore. Time and time again, case history writers do not achieve any balanced empathy with their two audiences.

However uneven the intrinsic and historical worth of Freud's case histories, they were at the center of most psychoanalytic teaching programs until the 1970s and remain so in many places today. If Freud's works traditionally constituted the basic canon of psychoanalysis, his five case histories were its Pentateuch, its Torah, its canon within the canon. Indeed, the privileged value attributed to Freud's cases has set psychoanalysis off from other sciences: although empirical data have a foundational role in psychoanalysis, the works of its founder, who died decades ago, continue to enjoy canonical status.

I have discussed elsewhere (1993a) the debate that has raged across disciplines, from literature to theology, about what writings should be honored as canonical or textually representative. In psychoanalysis, I explained, that debate has provoked three reactions. One tendency has been to denounce the fetishistic importance conferred upon Freud's cases and relegate them to a minor place in the curriculum. The spectacular progress of post-Freudian analysis on so many fronts, so the argument runs, should not be halted for the sake of antiquated case histories that tell little about the psychoanalytic process and the crucial minutiae of therapeutic interchange. Second, some contend that Freud's classic cases should be retained and spotlighted for subversive reasons—for example, to expose how psychoanalysts' interpretation of Freud is often symptomatic of their institutional disturbance, much as Freud's writing in his case histories is symptomatic of his countertransferential difficulties. Proponents would even insist that to achieve a more authentic picture of Freud's practice, some of his other analyses should also be taught, such as those of Howard Frink or Gizella Pálos, Sandor Ferenczi's patient-lover and the daughter of his mistress—analyses, in short, in which Freud's practice was highly questionable on moral grounds.

Those holding a third attitude toward Freud's case histories stress their positive qualities in several ways. A well-presented and engaging case history requires an analyst with scriptive talents, and Freud had them to an unsurpassed degree. His classic cases manifest a blending of associative and critical processes that transmits a flavor of the clinical situation; an empathic quality in object relationships (a feature often obliterated in Strachey's translation of Freud's writings); a powerful rhetorical interweaving of clinician, author, patient, and reader; a theoretical and expository sensitivity to language; and an ability to shift easily and quickly among many frames of reference. Freud's case histories can also serve as a privileged locus for scrutinizing his frequently misunderstood concepts, as well as for comparing, inter alia, the difference between Anglo-American and French interpretive traditions. Finally, let us remember that the vignette, whatever its popularity in current psychoanalytic literature, can illustrate, but not validate, theory; neither can the vignette, because of its discursive form, compare with the case history in providing a complex and in-depth account of treatment over a period of years.

This volume completes my trilogy on Freud's case histories. I have already published *The Cries of the Wolf Man* (1984), a radical revision of which appears in a French translation for the series Bibliothèque de la Psychanalyse, edited by Jean Laplanche (1995). My book *Freud and the Rat Man* (1986a) appeared in the same French series, but without revision. Both French editions contain dozens of substantial linguistic notes by the translator (and psychoanalyst) Bertrand Vichyn.

After I had written an analysis of Katharina (1989), Freud's most charming case history, the time became ripe for me to address the remaining case histories of Freud's female patients, I diverted from my main path to publish some new thoughts on little Hans (1993b); meanwhile, because of the unforeseen complexity of my general project, I decided to devote a separate volume to Dora and to leave Freud's other published female cases for a future date.

In recent times the Dora case has received a wave of critical attention from inside and outside psychoanalysis—a surprise in some ways, for classic hysteric symptomatology has now given yielded the spotlight to anorexia nervosa and other disturbances.

Commentators on Dora include analysts specializing in adolescent development and female psychology and representing such different schools as Lacanianism and self-psychology; literary critics addressing the complexities in narrative structure and figurative language; professionals in sociology, history, and political science; and feminists working in gender studies and in any other discipline. As a result, a refined awareness has emerged about nosology, transferential and countertransferential aspects in the case, and lastly, Dora's psychodynamics and their manifold social context. Feminists have proclaimed with good reason that the clinical deficiencies of the case, besides being indicative of Freud's pathology, are part and parcel of the subsequent pathological acceptance of the case by the psychological community. That is, a tradition of misreading has continued the clinical mismanagement.

Why, then, another study of Dora? In a narrow sense, the meetings between Dora and Freud—roughly seventy hours in all—do have a rich, though restricted, meaning. Yet those spots of time, by virtue of having been pored over by scholars from various fields, have expanded into a paradigmatic historical record both of psychoanalysis and, more importantly, of contemporary culture; thus aggrandized, the Dora case merits even more attention. But the case possesses, too, a panoramic scope coincident with human history itself, in that the treatment at 19 Berggasse was also a gender war engaging two subjects, woman and man. That panoramic scope will become clearer in the course of this book.

In bare outline, the Dora case seems conventional. Freud divides his presentation into five parts: a short, unnumbered section entitled "Prefatory Remarks"; chapter 1, "The Clinical Picture," a general history of the case interlarded with theoretical explanations; chapter 2, "The First Dream"; chapter 3, "The Second Dream"; and chapter 4, the "Postscript" containing Freud's famous discussion of transference. Mundane appearance notwithstanding, the case history of Dora harbors an astonishing complexity, and I have discovered something new each time I have returned to it. Freud's way of proceeding, of interspersing a

wealth of data with his own associations and investigations, challenges the exegete. Added to that, the ever-increasing amount of
scholarship on the case makes it by far the most discussed of
Freud's case histories and thereby augments the formidable task
awaiting any serious investigator. Some scholars have clarified the
historical content and context of Dora's case history. Helped by
unpublished data made available by Peter Loewenberg, Arnold
Rogow (1978, 1979) completed a pair of enlightening documen-
tary articles on Dora. Loewenberg has written up his own material
(1983), and closer to the present, Hannah Decker has written a
book on Dora (1991) that has furnished significant historical
background. Decker gives a detailed description of the persecu-
tion of Jews at the end of the nineteenth century in central Europe. In the part of the modern-day Czech Republic where Dora's
father had his factories, for example, Jewish homes and business
properties were subject to arson.

Supplementing that new historical material with my own
archival research, I have subjected the case history to an exeget-
ical and psychoanalytic examination that goes beyond previous
studies. In the pages to follow, readers will recurrently come upon
cardinal features of the German text that have been lost in English; some of those I have already offered to the forthcoming
Revised Standard Edition of Freud's works. In Chapter 1, I reframe
the oft-told story about Freud's immortal patient, introduce some
of the problems besetting the case history, initiate a leitmotif of
linguistic elucidation, and provide, in closing, an amplified chronological table. In Chapter 2, I begin my exposition, augmented in
subsequent chapters, of Fliess as a major protagonist in the Dora
case; I then depict Freud's hitherto-untold theoretical and personal struggles with bisexuality, and I clarify Freud's historical
understanding of transference. In Chapter 3, I expose the wealth
of contradictions and hasty assumptions made by Freud as he
reconstructed the development of Dora's trauma and symptoms. I
suggest that Freud's unempathic expectations of how Dora should
have reacted to her trauma contrasts with his subsequent protec-
tiveness of his own adolescent daughter before the sexually ad-

venturous Jones. Drawing on modern developments in psychoanalysis, I also provide an updated diagnostic account of Dora's psychopathology.

In Chapter 4, I discuss meanings obfuscated in the English translation of Dora's two dreams, situate the dreams in their temporal context, show their complementary nature, uncover imagistic motifs, and relate the dreams in revelatory ways to Dora's psychopathology. In Chapter 5, I locate the Dora case history within Freud's general practice of case-history writing that features an erotics of narrative enactment, then I scrutinize an array of other discursive elements, ranging from gendered subtext and polysemous language to phonetic artistry and overdetermined imagery. In the concluding chapter, my summary statements are supplemented by further psychoanalytic reflections of a historical and textual order.

Acknowledgments

I am grateful to the following people and institutions for their assistance: Karl Heinz Baumeister, director of the Vorarlberger Landesarchiv; the Czech Consulate in Montreal and the Ministry of the Interior of the Czech Republic; Walter Pagler (Vienna); Wolfgang Mayer and his colleagues in the Wiener Stadt- und Landesarchiv Magistratsabteilung; Hans Jäger-Sunstenau (Vienna); Hubert Kiem of Ufficio Anagrafe (Merano); Federicio Steinhaus, president of the Comunità Ebraica (Merano); Mimi Chugani of the Austrian Trade Commission (Montreal); Janice Holland and François Gagnon (Montreal); Heidi Weiss of the Israelitische Kultusgemeinde (Vienna); Christa Aldrian of the Österreichischen Nationalbibliothek (Vienna); Eva Nikki of the Museum für angewandte Kunst (Vienna); and Lydia Marinelli of the Sigmund Freud-Gesellschaft (Vienna).

A work like mine has other indebtedness: to patients, students, colleagues. In particular, let me thank Jean Bossé, André Clas, Ernst Falzeder, Gerhard Fichtner, Albrecht Hirschmüller, Hans Israels, Peter Loewenberg, and Hans-Herbert Räkel. Janice Stuart was helpful, kind, and assiduous; and Alex Ferguson guided me through the magical land of the computer. The present book is my fourth that has benefited from the acuity of Gladys Topkis, my editor at Yale University Press. Mary Pasti, my manuscript editor, has been exemplary in her attentiveness and perceptiveness.

Special mention must once more be made of Pierrette, whose love has taught me gratitude and the joyful freedom that goes with it.

Finally, I want to express my heartfelt thanks to the Killam Foundation for its generous support of this book and my other writings during the same period.

Freud's Dora

1

Steering the Story

Now I shall be accused of giving information.

For better and for worse, Sigmund Freud's longest text on a female patient, the case history of Dora, has become part of our psychoanalytic and non-psychoanalytic heritage. To start with a positive litany, the case history of Dora has been called the first of Freud's great analytic cases and the first involving an adolescent; the centerpiece of Freud's memorable trilogy, bounded by *The Interpretation of Dreams* (1900) and *Three Essays on the Theory of Sexuality* (1905); "a model for students of psychoanalysis" (Jones, 1955, 257); and "the classical analysis of the structure and the genesis of a hysteria" (Erikson, 1964, 169–170). Besides providing a canonic specimen of conversion hysteria and being Freud's last clinical write-up of hysteria, it has been hailed as his most graphic demonstration of psychosomatics; a pioneering exposition of the therapeutic significance of dreams, oral sexuality and bisexuality, and the role of fixation; a landmark in the evolution of psychoanalytic theory and technique; a key historical chapter on the reception of psychoanalysis; and his clinical document most

The epigraphs for the chapters are from the Dora case, except the one for Chapter 5, which is from Freud, 1985.
References to the Dora text, found in Freud's *Gesammelte Werke*, or *G.W.*, volume 5 (1952), and the *Standard Edition*, or *S.E.*, volume 7 (1905a), are indicated by page numbers separated by a slash. A citation of just one number refers to *S.E.* unless otherwise indicated. I shall sometimes take the liberty of referring to Strachey as a shorthand way of talking about *S.E.* or about Strachey and the set of translators collaborating with him.

discussed in sociology, anthropology, history, and literary criticism, as well as psychiatry and psychoanalysis.

If one panel of Dora's diptych shows positive characterizations, the other bears these running captions: one of the remarkable psychoanalytic failures and a model for teaching what not to do technically; a testament not just to Freud's creative genius but also to his reckless tracing of symptomatology to its unconscious sources; a stereotypical illustration of the male misconception of woman's social exclusion and, in particular, an inkblot test of Freud's fantasized misapprehensions about female sexuality and adolescence. In the annals of Western culture, Dora has emerged as a paradigmatic example of how patriarchal forces in the nineteenth century—political, social, and medical—oppressed a Jewish girl who had to write out her pain in her body.

The uniqueness of Dora's case history as a historical document prompts us to visit its lived details. Thanks to Freud, we know the subject more through her alias than through her real-life name, Ida Bauer. Reflecting the etymology of the name he gave her (which means "gifts" in Greek), Dora was fated to be an object of exchange. She opened her eyes for the first time in Vienna toward the close of the nineteenth century. Although in the beginning of his case history Freud wrote that analysts should attend as much to "the purely human and social circumstances of patients as to the somatic data and the symptoms of the disorder" (18), he either downplayed or disregarded entirely the burden of Dora as a woman, a Jew, and an adolescent victimized by two pairs of adults. We had to gather from other sources that Dora grew up in a bourgeois Bohemian family of assimilated Jews who identified with German culture.[1] By all reports, her mother, Käthe (the shortened form of Katharina) was uncultivated, controlling, and insensitive to her children's talents. Her concern over her own constipation also helped crowd out any consideration for those around her, provoking Dora's merciless criticism.

---

1. For the social background of the Jews in nineteenth-century central Europe, the works of Decker (1991) and Gilman (1991) are excellent.

Freud described Käthe as having a "housewife's psychosis," so we are not taken aback to learn that her obsession with cleaning prevented domestic articles from being used, let alone enjoyed. Though telling, the particulars about Käthe remain sparse. If she zealously scoured her house, Freud thoroughly wiped her out of his case history. I should also point out an etymological irony: the name Käthe comes from the Greek word *katharos*, meaning "pure" or "clean"; the woeful woman might well not have known the link between her name and the cognate *katharsis*, "purgation." But such linguistic facts would not have escaped Freud, who wrote a journal in Greek as a student and who could cite passages of Greek poetry well into his adulthood.

Seen through Freud's dark lens and compared with his wife, Philip Bauer seems to shine in some ways—but no merit accrues to the one-eyed man who is king among the blind (the comparison is particularly apt because he was sightless in one eye). A wealthy textile manufacturer, he could impress with his shrewdness and perspicacity. But he appeared crippled in both body and mind—and reportedly was impotent. Sickly as a youth, Philip underwent a series of serious maladies in middle age. He was also given to hypocrisy and self-serving secrecy; he preferred "deviousness and a roundabout way."[2] Philip's premarital syphilis in every way affected relations with his wife, and he transmitted it to her as part of an unexpected dowry. His later gift of pearl drops for her ears was also unforgettable for the quarrel it occasioned.

After marrying Philip, Käthe quickly had her two children, Otto and, fourteen months later, the tormented heroine of our story. It is not surprising to learn that in a household beset with psychic and physical ailments, both Otto and Dora often fell ill in their childhood and had protracted periods of bedwetting. In other respects the young Otto possessed traits that had implications for the future: he exhibited brilliance, and he tended to stay out of family disputes. When forced to participate, he took his

---

2. By not translating "deviousness" (*krumm*), Strachey tones down the double criticism in *einen krummen Umweg*, 282/118.

mother's side, except in one notable instance: he called for his mother and his sister to accept Philip's philandering, which betokened his inhibited aggression in later political life. Dora, in contrast, revolted.

Although Otto Bauer became a well-known public figure, we have learned little about his early or private life. His personal reserve was motivated by political concerns as well as by an abiding embroilment with his intrusive mother. Yet his passive reaction to her, along with a readiness to deny and to rationalize, would serve to undercut his resolve in the professional arena. Two poignant stories have survived which testify to Otto's passivity toward his mother. She had the habit of opening all the windows to air out the house, even in the height of winter. Once a cousin came upon Otto studying in his room and dressed in overcoat, hat, and gloves. When asked why he didn't close the window, Otto replied: "But, after all, it's not so bad." The other bit of family lore is that Käthe, who possessed the sole key to a number of rooms in the family apartment, performed a nightly ritual of locking up the salon, where Philip kept his cigars, and the dining room, which provided the sole entrance to and exit from Otto's bedroom. In short, Otto submitted to his mother's policy of open windows and closed doors.

Unlike Käthe, whose compulsiveness appears quasi-psychotic, her humorless son had the traits of a more integrated obsessional. Somewhat "effeminate" gestures and unkempt dress point up Otto's filial ambivalence toward his mother. His maternal attachment continued beyond early life and left an imprint on his political speeches, wherein he had a habit of referring to the sacrifice of mothers rather than of fathers. Only after his parents' deaths did Otto marry and then, like his father, take a mistress. But I suspect that this oedipal identification was more complicated: Philip was nine years older than his wife; Otto selected a wife ten years his senior and, in reverse, chose a mistress ten years younger than himself.

If society helped drive Dora into the net of sexual intrigue and into the plight of her sex, it favored (though did not fully determine) Otto's rigidity in the more intellectual cast of an obsessional neurosis. Playing out their divided fate, Otto made an escape into the male-appropriate activity of politics, much as his sister did into illness, taking her credits under the footlights of the public stage, where lurked the deep shadows of family gloom. Nearly monomaniacally devoted to politics and writing, Otto achieved eminence as parliamentary leader and foreign minister of the First Austrian Republic, as its chief Marxist theorist, and as secretary to the Austrian Social Democratic Workers' Party. He preached violence in his radical theory, but he tempered his rebellion against the powerful paternal rulers and hesitated to defend the impotent workers. Continuing the compromise formations established in the family of his youth, he carried out his political functions with a mixture of moral austerity, theoretical brilliance, indecisiveness in practice, and charismatic inspiration.

Dora was born in 32 Berggasse, not far from the house that the Freud family would inhabit nine years later. Another serendipitous fact is that while Dora was seeing Freud, she lived on Lichtensteinstrasse, the same street on which Anna O. once resided. Both women became the subjects of unforgettable clinical narratives.

In conformity with Freud's biological theory of humankind as a primal boy, Dora's succumbing to asthma at the age of eight divided her early life into two distinct phases. The first was that of a wild boy with the ability to masturbate herself to breathless orgasm; the second, that of a sick, well-behaved girl: "In Dora's case the masturbation had remained undiscovered and had come to an end in an instant. . . . It was as though she had been a boy up till that moment and then had become girlish for the first time. She had in truth been a wild creature [*ein wildes Ding*]; but after the 'asthma' she became quiet and well behaved. That illness formed the boundary between two phases of her sexual life, of which the first was masculine in character and the second feminine" (243–244n/81–82n).[3] Under the cover of Freud's gendered

3. On the citation system see the note on page 1. A full study of Freud's

account of Dora's first memories, we can recast her early metamorphosis this way: he-she was sucking a thumb and meanwhile
pulling at Otto's earlobe. Thereafter he-she continued thumb-
sucking and bedwetting for some time. Because the parents' bedroom was just next door and they copulated within earshot, he-
she was also given to masturbation. So it came to pass, according
to the word of Freud, that upon her second beginning, Dora
breathed out heavily and became she. The asthma, in Freud's
lights, served as a psychosomatic midwife for Dora's entrance into
demure femininity. Man unmade.

Looking into the immediate background, we find that just two
years before Dora got asthma her father contracted tuberculosis.
He then moved with his family to Merano, a health resort 250
miles southwest of Vienna. Its visitors included Arthur Schnitzler
(1882–1885), Rainer Maria Rilke (1897), Christian Morgenstern
(1906), Stefan Zweig (1908), and Freud, as well as Freud's daughter Anna. When the Bauers lived in Merano, there was only one
school for girls, directed by the Kloster der englischen Fräulein.
Contrary to published account, Dora did not attend that school,
and I can only assume that a governess educated her at home, a
circumstance setting her off from Otto, who had the social mobility
of a male, and testifying to her domestic imprisonment.[4]

Another family resident in Merano, the Zellenkas, offered a
mixed kind of friendship to the Bauers. I suspect that Freud's
designations for the Zellenka couple—Herr and Frau K.—derive

---

gender biases has yet to be completed. He told his Viennese colleagues that
"neurotics turn activity into passivity, so that a neurotic man could in fact be called
feminine" (Nunberg and Federn, 1962, 237). R. Davis has written a comprehen-
sive analysis of how Freud understood the gender-charged concept of passivity.
Davis concludes: "Before Freud began to develop his psychology of women in
1925, his extensive linking of the terms passive and feminine was almost exclusively in discussions of masculine psychology" (1993, 171).

4. The erroneous information is in Decker, 1991, 154, 230. I am grateful to
the Merano nuns, who conducted an exhaustive search in the archives. They had
no student named Ida Bauer in the 1890s. Were the facts otherwise, it would have
been too good to be true, for in that the name of the nuns' order in English is the
Institute of the Blessed Virgin Mary, their imprint would have influenced Dora's
meditating on Raphael's Sistina Madonna for two hours.

from the last syllable in the family name (Germans pronounce the letter *k* as "kah"). The husband, Hans, whose birthdate cannot be ascertained, came from the region of Ledeč in Bohemia; his wife, Peppina (the shortened form of Guiseppina), was born in Ancona, Italy, in 1870. The couple married in Merano in 1889, and both of their children were born in 1891, Otto at the beginning of the year and Clara at the end.[5]

Much less wealthy than Philip, who was the owner of a textile empire abroad, Hans ran his business at 4 Habsburgstrasse, on Merano's main street, today called Freiheitstrasse. The Zellenkas had their own physical problems: Peppina was overcome by "nervous disorders" (33) and became unable to walk, so she had to spend several months in a sanatorium; and Clara, a congenitally ill daughter, would die at age nine. The warm climate in Merano tendered its own clouded blessing to the Bauers: during Philip's absence from home for the first time since his health improved, his daughter suffered her first asthmatic attack, after which she was made to rest for six months (21).

Other misfortunes followed. On top of learning that her father had had a premarital "illness," Dora saw him beset by a detached retina in his one functioning eye, and she carried out light nursing duties for him. Her brother, Otto, graphically recalled how his father was forced to lie in a darkened room for weeks on end; he described the experience as the "most impressive" of his childhood.

In 1894, Dora witnessed her father undergoing his gravest affliction—a confusional attack, followed by paralysis and some minor mental disturbances. Meanwhile, although tending her father, Dora herself was suffering from her historically memorable cough, which could last for weeks and cause complete loss of

---

5. Peppina was born in Ancona on March 20, 1870; she was the daughter of Isidor Heumann (1826–1893) and Jeanette Biedermann. Hans was the son of Ignatz Zellenka and Charlotte Spiegel. Hans and Peppina married in Merano on September 22, 1889. Otto was born on January 5, 1891, and Clara on December 26 of the same year (for this information I am grateful to Karl Burmeister, director of the Landesarchiv Voralberg, located in Bregenz, Austria).

voice. Her distress was complicated by her sympathetic imitation of her sick father and her display of his contagiousness. With this double message Dora's cough "called out into the world."[6] In the same year, Hans Zellenka took Philip to consult Freud, who rendered a diagnosis of taboparesis and prescribed an antisyphilitic treatment. Fatefully, Dora began to be supplanted by Peppina, who first nursed Philip, then loved him. Did Philip offer a reparative opportunity to Peppina, who still mourned the death of her father the previous year? And did the fact that Philip, too, had a son named Otto make her feel allied to him?

Each adult has leisure time in one way or another. Käthe showed no interest in her children's more active concerns, whereas Peppina showed only "slight" interest in her children (37), including the congenitally ill Clara. Peppina enjoyed taking care of Philip, who showered her with gifts. Hans, in turn, gave caring gifts to Dora, including a memorable jewel case. He appears to have regarded maids and young women as disposable or recyclable sex objects; he was given a free hand with Dora and used it—a circumstance it is time to discuss.

Dora underwent her first sexual trauma in Hans's place of business. Hans had arranged to be alone with Dora on the pretext that the upper balconies of the house where he had his shop, less than two hundred feet from the Sandplatz, afforded a convenient view of the spectacular church procession to take place (probably in celebration of a feast day). Key points along the route were the Sandplatz and another main square, the Domplatz (Cathedral Square; but actually the church on the square, Saint Nicolaus, is not a cathedral). Hans asked that while he closed the outside shutters Dora await him at a door at the back of the house that opened onto a staircase leading to the upper balconies. He came back to where she stood at the back door, and there he clasped the unsuspecting thirteen-year-old Dora to him and then kissed her.

Revolted, she wrenched herself away and fled, mentioning

---

6. "Rief . . . in die Welt hinaus," 194/82, my italics. Strachey's less dynamic "proclaimed out loud" captures the note of externalization, not entrance.

the incident to no one at the time. Freud later downplayed the episode as the "little scene" of a "thumb-sucker" (51, 74), thrice upgrading Dora to fourteen. And he also made Dora older for us by saying that one year (instead of two) had elapsed between the little scene and her subsequent erotic trauma when she was nearly sixteen. We should also note Freud's erratic slippage in developmental designations when he depicts Dora's little scene: "Herr K. had arranged with her [Dora] and his wife that the ladies [*Damen*; compare *S.E.*: 'they'] should go in the afternoon to his shop on the main square. . . . He convinced his wife, however, to remain at home; he sent his clerks away and was alone when the girl [*Mädchen*] came into his place of business. . . . He suddenly pulled the girl to him and pressed a kiss on her lips. . . . The behavior of the fourteen-year-old child [*Kind*] was already entirely and completely hysterical" (186–187/28, my translation).

According to Freud's construction of the incident, the invited lady turns into a visiting girl whose panic suits her as a hysterical child. Earlier in Freud's gender-biased devolutionary schema, Dora had changed from a masturbatory male to an asthmatic female; now she descended from ladyhood to girlhood to childhood and from polite complaisance to immature panic.

A homemade recipe went into the next sequence of Freud's story: take two families, each beset with physical sickness, internal turmoil, and sexual strife; mix the principals together, bring to a boil, let simmer, and add spicy condiments as desired. Philip and Peppina carried on their intense liaison, Käthe her intense affair with cleaning. But the otherwise disparate wives resembled each other in their strategic relapses into illness as a way of avoiding sex with their mates. Peppina in particular grew healthy when Hans was away on business trips but, more often than chance would have it, became ill upon his return. Musical illnesses: Dora could develop aphonia when the ever-attentive Hans was away (he often wrote to tell her rather than his wife when he would return), and Philip simulated sickness in order to vacation with Peppina.

Dora had little chance for normal growth in an interfamilial soap opera whose quartet of adults were exploiting her and denying that exploitation. She swirled in a maelstrom of treachery whose partners, down on their luck, wanted her as one of their lesser number—a continuation of the exploitation of children, especially females, that prevailed within both the patriarchal social system and the family circle. Philip, to compensate for the presents that he gave to Peppina, was also generous to his wife and daughter. Many of his gifts for Dora were even chosen by Peppina. (It is worth remarking that the German word *Gift* means "poison" in English.) Much as Philip handed over his syphilitic infection to his wife, he handed over his daughter to Hans as a kind of consolation prize, swapping his daughter for his neighbor's wife.

The game's name was intrigue; one aim was the service and servitude of Dora's body. Under the eyes of all, Hans tended to his charge and her role in an erotic circuit. He tendered costly presents, passed all his spare time in her company, and for a whole year even sent her flowers every day.

There was more. When her role as confidante to her father was taken over by Peppina, Dora saw that altruistic surrender stood no direct chance against erotic surrender. She opted for next best: she became Peppina's confidante in her unhappy married life. (What were the fantasies of this married woman who selected her lover's young daughter to share the most intimate details in her life?) Not only did Dora refrain from criticizing Peppina, but she loved her "adorable white body" (61); and when Dora stayed with the Zellenkas, she shared a bedroom with Peppina while Hans slept elsewhere. In no way could Dora ascribe her troubles to Peppina as their "prime originator" (*Urheberin*, 222/62, my translation).[7] As a tender nurse to the Zellenkas' two children, Dora even acted as an accomplice: she facilitated her father's affair, to the point of diverting the children to walk away from the romancing pair. All became locked into dealings and wheelings that spoke out in various directions.

7. The rendering "prime author" in *S.E.* has prevented commentators from connecting Peppina with Freud's own nannie, or *Urheberin*, translated as "prime originator" (Freud, 1986, 288/1985, 268). See also Freud's account of his incestuous dream about his daughter Mathilde, where he labels a father an *Urheber*, this time translated simply as "originator" (1986, 266/1985, 249).

Freud, for his part, presses ahead, listing Dora's age at a traumatic lake scene as sixteen instead of fifteen. I suspect that the lake is the Lago di Garda, the favorite summer resort for the residents of Merano, which was just sixty miles to the north.[8] Just before accompanying Dora to the lake, Philip took her to see Freud, who deemed the hoarse, coughing girl to be "unmistakably neurotic"; but nothing more came of the meeting, for the symptoms went away by themselves. While at the lake, Dora learned from the Zellenkas' governess that Hans, while "ardently courting" the governess (*sehr umwerben*, 268/105, my translation), had complained, "I get nothing out of my wife." Hans used the same sexual allusion shortly afterward when, pressing his suit, he made an overture of love to Dora (26, 106).[9]

Insulted and traumatized by Hans's approach, Dora slapped him in the face and fled. That afternoon she took a nap in her room, only to awaken and find Hans beside her, insisting that he could go into his room whenever it suited him. The next day Dora wanted to take the precaution of undressing behind the locked door of her room; this time, however, the key was missing. That night Dora had her famous dream about a burning house and dreamed it again over the next two nights. Then she abruptly cut short her stay at the summer resort, not wanting to be without her father, who had planned to be there for only a few days. Hard pressed, Hans requested Dora not to let the cat out of the bag (more about that later) by mentioning his pursuit; previously, let us note, Hans had often spoken bitterly to Käthe about her husband's affair with Peppina.

Other consequences of the lake scene were more dramatic, if not much more painful. After Dora accused Hans of making indecent advances, her father wrote to him and asked for an

8. When Dora walked along the lake for two and a half hours, she was at the northern part of Lago di Garda.
9. Strachey translates this as "made violent love," an expression that today refers to hostile physical passion rather than courting. I deliberately translate *Liebesantrag* (184/25) with the ambiguous "overture of love" in order to render the seductive blur between a proposal and a proposition. In *S.E.*, Hans's action is the ameliorative "proposal." Elsewhere Strachey uses "proposal" to translate *Werbung* (235/73, 257/95, 268/106), which is rather "wooing" or "courting."

explanation. Hans protested sentiments of the highest esteem for her. A few weeks later, when Philip called him to account in Merano, there was no longer any question of esteem. Hans brought up charges of delusion. He spoke of Dora with disparagement and produced as his trump card the suggestion that no girl who read erotic books could have any title to a man's respect. Dora realized that Peppina must have been the source of that treacherous slander, for only with her did Dora read Mantegazza's *Physiology of Love* and discuss forbidden topics.

Turning turncoat once more, Hans made another overture to Dora that Christmas. Meanwhile, Dora's mental landscape altered: she tottered into depression and now impugned her father instead of facilitating his relationship with Peppina. When Dora complained about Hans's erotic advances, Philip, according prime importance to his own cavorting with Peppina, found refuge in the charge that fictions grew in Dora's mind. The adults now colluded in denial of Dora's sexual abuse. Käthe's share was to sugarcoat: she told a fairy tale about how Peppina had saved Philip from suicide by reminding him of his familial obligations. Dora found herself in a snare of lies and betrayal constructed by two married couples. On all sides they boxed her in, a commodified object—worse still, damaged goods.

Not long after the death of her favorite aunt the following year, Dora developed constipation, fever, and symptoms of appendicitis. In the same year the Bauers moved from Merano to the Bohemian town of Reichenberg (now Liberec), nearly two hundred miles northwest of Vienna but closer to Philip's two textile plants. It was in Reichenberg that Dora successfully argued for the dismissal of her governess who resembled Peppina in loving Dora not for her own sake but for love of Philip. Before long, the Bauers relocated in Vienna, and three weeks later the Zellenkas made their move to the same city. Once more Dora could not rely on any one adult to protect her. In the major geographical sites of her young life—Vienna, Merano, the lakeside resort, and Reichenberg—we feel that Dora did not enjoy any of the fresh air of altruism.

The psychological and sociological strictures of a male-dominated society facilitated Dora's plunge into hysterical torment and hampered her intellectual growth. Her depressive symptoms culminated in fainting and convulsion when her father reproved her sometime after finding the suicide note that she apparently left lying about to be discovered. Although he had reached the end of his own devices with his daughter, Philip would not honor any request that he sever relations with the Zellenkas. Hydrotherapy and electrical treatments by various physicians produced no positive result. The impasse moved him to take Dora, coughing and appearing lame, to Freud, who was also acquainted with other sick members in the family circle. But angling to maintain the status quo, Philip pled at 19 Berggasse: "Please try and bring her to reason" (read: "nonreason"). Philip's version of the "talking cure" (*Redekur*) was for Freud to talk Dora out (*ausreden*, 272/109) of her suspicions. He disregarded his daughter's victimization and wanted only that she would groan no more.

Freud gives Dora the age of eighteen and reports the analysis as lasting for three months.[10] Her symptomatology represented a compromise formation of protest against exploitation that increased her helplessness and victimization. She presented herself to Freud in the latter part of her coughing spell, which, together with the first part, which entailed aphonia, lasted from three to six weeks. While narrating the history of her ailments she added that her mother's and her own catarrh originated as "transferences" of her father's venereal disease.[11] Yet the absence of spectacular symptoms continued to convince Freud, ever since their first meeting, that Dora had merely a minor hysteria. He was also struck by her qualities and attitudes: independent judgment, an

10. Elsewhere Freud says that Dora was "nearly nineteen" (cf. 16, 18, 20, 22, and 51); we know, however, that for the first weeks of the treatment, Dora was still seventeen. Freud also asserts that the treatment lasted somewhat less than three months (cf. 10, 11, 12, 14, and 115). Jones's description (1953, 362) of the treatment as continuing for eleven weeks would therefore have it start in mid-October and accordingly last two and a half months.

11. The verb *übertragen*, 247/84; compare *S.E.*: "handed on to."

active interest in women's rights, mockery of physicians, a lifelong bitterness toward her mother, and a relatively recent resentment of her father. Within this general picture her intellectual gifts as well as her disposition to illness seemed to have come from her father's side of the family.

Over the hours of their meeting, Freud conducted himself in an adversarial manner that sometimes approached the brutal. If anything, his grilling increased her resistances. Freud even proposed that yielding to Hans would have been the best solution "for all parties concerned" (108). His solution, in other words, was that she submit to a male-empowering ménage à quatre and accept herself as a female object, fashioned to male devices—El Dorado. We might think that our pathetic subject could have been no match for Freud, a forty-four-year-old genius functioning at the height of his intellectual powers and well settled in family life with six children of his own. But contest there was, and little therapy. Fate spoiled the battle and plundered from both sides.

The rest of the story offers little solace to lovers of happy endings. After treatment Dora sank into a temporary muddle before feeling better, and her father visited Freud a few times. In May 1901 the death of young Clara Zellenka occasioned a visit of condolence by Dora, during which both Zellenkas owned up to their previously denied erotic designs. That fall Dora incurred an attack of aphonia upon seeing Hans knocked down by a carriage. In April 1902, two weeks after reading about Freud's appointment to a professorship, Dora consulted Freud about a facial neuralgia that she had developed. Besides doubting her sincerity, Freud understood her neuralgia as a self-punishment for having left him and for having slapped Hans four years earlier.

In 1903, Dora married Ernst Adler, nine years her senior; the age discrepancy is identical to that between her mother and father. Unsuccessful as a musician, her husband accepted a position in Dora's father's employ. In 1905 she bore her only child, a boy, whom she named Kurt Hubert; the same year she and her husband converted to Protestantism. Freud's case history was also published in 1905. So shaken was Freud by Dora that he distorted the truth in the preface to the case history—we can detect this from contrary statements made in his private correspondence at the time. Freud claimed that he waited to publish his report until a change came upon Dora, yet we know (as we shall see later in detail) that he immediately and unsuccessfully tried to put the case in print. He claimed, too, that one other doctor knew about the case, yet there were two—Wilhelm Fliess and Oscar Rie (as we shall also see later in detail).

Although I shall examine Fliess's relevance for the Dora case in later chapters, a few pertinent facts may now suffice: both Fliess and Dora figured centrally and simultaneously in Freud's conflicts over bisexuality; those conflicts entered the correspondence between Fliess and Freud about the ongoing case and its write-up; the name of Fliess (which means "flow" in German) is covertly present in the remarkable abundance of liquid imagery flooding the case history; Freud had the same reason for disliking Dora and Fliess's wife, and the two women had the same real first name. Although Fliess was mentioned in the case history for his nasal treatment for gastralgia, he never met Dora, and this leads us to the next sequence of her story.

In 1923 an attending otolaryngologist decided to ask Felix Deutsch to diagnose the bedridden Dora, for it was suspected that her symptoms of Ménière's disease—including a ringing in the right ear—had a psychic origin. Deutsch suggested that Dora's symptoms related to her waiting up at night for the return of her grown son, who she suspected had become interested in girls. Impressed by the interpretation, Dora asked for another consultation. The next and last time Deutsch saw Dora, she was out of bed and declaring that her attacks had passed.

All in all, along with the persistence of her childhood limp, dyspnea, and periodic migraines, Dora reported to Deutsch other complaints: premenstrual pains, vaginal discharge, and frigidity. While continuing to admire her brother, Otto, she railed against her neglecting mother, displayed a paranoid sense of revenge against men, and said her husband was unfaithful. Like her mother, who saw dirt in herself and in her surroundings, Dora suffered from constipation and a compulsion to clean. Otto called on Deutsch several times afterward and brought up his sister's lack of confidence in others and her turning them against each other. Years later, an informant told Deutsch that Dora was "one of the most repulsive hysterics he had ever met" (Deutsch, 1957, 167).

Deutsch's article on Freud's case history (1957), which aims in great part both to exonerate Freud and to laud his perspicacity, must be read with many grains of salt. It contains numerous factual errors, putting into doubt its reliability about substantial issues. For example, Deutsch places the interviews in the fall of 1922, whereas extant evidence points to their occurrence in March 1923; he misdates Otto's death, gives the wrong age for Dora at the time of the interview, and misrepresents her mother and father as living; and he quotes one of Freud's reflections in the case history and puts it in the mouth of Dora. In subtle and not so subtle ways Deutsch continues Freud's dismissive and critical portrait of Dora. By entitling his article a "footnote" to Freud's case Deutsch reflects his submissive role and passes off his report as an afterthought. Whereas he says in his essay that Dora was proud to be the subject of Freud's case history, he wrote to his estranged wife, Helene, in April 1923 that Dora had "nothing good to say about analysis." Such was the unwitting power of Dora, however frail in body, to provoke two physicians, the private and public Freud, and then the private and public Deutsch, into making contradictory statements about her.[12]

For Dora herself, Fate turned the wheel once more. Between the world wars, contract bridge became the social craze in Vienna, and bridge teachers were in demand. Far different from Hans, who had played a metaphorical trump card against her, Dora

12. For the quotation from Felix Deutsch's letter to Helene as well as for the date of his interviews with Dora, I am indebted to Paul Roazen's article (1994). On the basis of cogent internal evidence in Deutsch's contemporary correspondence, Roazen dates Deutsch's meetings with Dora to 1923, a year later than the date that Deutsch remembered.

became a real bridge master, with none other than Peppina as her partner.[13] She died in 1945.

> One sitting 'cross the other though now gamefully
> together, 'gainst another set of hands.
> A round and a
> round
> and around . . .

Chronology

If readers dwell on the following tabularized details, they will be better equipped to contend with the challenging intricacy of Dora's epic. The formatted chronicle, informative in its own right, serves also as a reference guide for readers who will want to resituate the various modifications and additions to Dora's narrative that I shall deliver in dosages in the chapters ahead.

1853 Ida's (Dora's) father, Philip Bauer, is born on August 14. (Bauer means "farmer" or "peasant" in German.)

1856 Philip's sister, Malvine, is born on January 6.

1862 Dora's mother, Katharina (Käthe) Gerber is born. (Gerber means "tanner" in German.)

1879 Käthe, age seventeen, and Philip, age twenty-six, are engaged.

1881 Käthe and Philip marry (was Käthe already pregnant?). Philip was syphilitic at the time. Their son, Otto, is born on September 5.

13. Decker, 1991, 175–176. For the social background to the Dora case, Decker's book is invaluable. Another source for the renewed friendship between Dora and Peppina is in the International Institute for Social History. Amsterdam (for this information I am grateful to Hans Israels). In the 1930s the Nazis were trying to track down Dora, because she was the sister of a well-known socialist leader; in flight, Dora stayed over with Peppina. Again they were accomplices, but now against the Nazis.

1882 Dora is born on November 1. According to Freud's mistaken report, Malvine "was a little older" than Philip (19).

1884 Dora later remembers herself at age one and a half at her nurse's breast.

1886 or 1887 Dora stops sucking her thumb.

1888 Philip contracts tuberculosis at age thirty-five. The Bauer family moves from Vienna to B——, actually the Tyrolean town of Merano.[14] There the Bauers meet the "K.'s" Hans and Peppina Zellenka.[15]

1889 Dora's bedwetting resumes at age seven.

1890 Dora is putatively exposed to the primal scene. A little later, her enuresis ceases with the onset of her first asthmatic attack, which lasts six months (according to Freud, Dora's neurotic symptoms begin only with the asthma, 21). After that illness, she takes her sick paternal aunt as her model.

1892 or 1893 Philip's retina becomes detached. Dora learns that her father was "ill" [syphilitic] before marriage.

1893 Peppina's father dies.

1894 Philip suffers his gravest illness, a confusional attack followed by paralysis. He begins his intimacy with Peppina Zellenka. Accompanied by Hans, Philip makes his first visit to Freud.

1896 The Bauers have a big argument about a piece of jewelry. According to the case history (68), Dora places the parental argument four years prior to her analytic treatment, but she also dates it as occurring "a year before the dream," near the lake, which would date the quarrel to 1897.
Dora is kissed by Hans (the "shop trauma"). Thrice Freud tells us that Dora was fourteen at the time of Hans's kiss

14. This fact was revealed for the first time by Rogoff (1979, 242). I am also indebted to Rogoff (1978, 1979) for the following information on Otto's political character, the date and nature of Philip's visual disturbances, and the occupational fate of Dora's husband.

15. Decker (1991, 65, 230) wrongly says that Hans was born in Merano.

(28). That dating is put into doubt by a remark elsewhere that the kiss scene occurred a year earlier than the lake scene, whose assured dating is 1898; the discrepancy was corrected by Freud in the editions of case history published in 1924 and thereafter (74). In a visit to Merano, I determined that the church in the main square, the still extant Saint Nicolaus, was the site of outside processions, which could have taken place in late April (in celebration of spring), on June 6 (the feast of the Sacred Heart of Christ), or on August 15 (the feast of the Assumption of the Blessed Virgin). In that the wealthy Bauers left Merano for their summer holidays, Dora's trauma must have taken place either at the end of April or in mid-June, when Dora was about thirteen and a half years old.[16]

1898 Peppina Zellenka invites Dora to a lake resort. On the way there, Philip, with his hoarse, coughing, "unmistakably neurotic" daughter, consults Freud. On June 30, Hans makes his sexual overture at the lakeside (the "lake trauma"). On the night of the following day and on the two nights thereafter, Dora has a dream about a burning house. On the fifth day after the lake scene, she leaves the resort with her father (67).[17]

That Christmas, Hans redeclares his intentions when presenting Dora a letter case (*Briefschachtel,* 271n/108n).

1899 Malvine Friedmann, Dora's favorite aunt, dies in April (not the winter of 1898, as assumed in *S.E.*, 6). Dora goes to Vienna after (not before) the death of her aunt (22).[18] During the Bauers' transitional residence in Reichenberg,

---

16. If indeed the shop trauma occurred on the feast of Corpus Christi (June 6, 1896), it was shortly before the Zellenka family moved from 8 Domplatz to 6 Habsburgstrasse, the house next to Hans's shop.

17. In an elliptical remark that does not fit well with Aunt Malvine's death and the Bauers' move from Merano the next year, Freud writes: "When, for the first time after Dora had broken off her stay by the lake, her father was going back to B——, she had naturally refused to go with him" (61).

18. This fact is overlooked by Decker (1991, 80): "It is not clear when she actually arrived, but she seems to have been there by February or March of 1899."

Dora finally causes the governess to be dismissed. According to Decker, the Bauers return to Vienna after staying in Reichenberg for a few months in 1899;[19] but Freud states that the Bauers move to Reichenberg in the fall (of 1899) and go on to Vienna "scarcely a year later" (22–23).

1900 Three weeks after the Bauers move to Vienna, the Zellenkas settle there. Dora, in her struggle against collapse, writes a suicide letter. Sometime after that, Philip visits Freud on several occasions (26) and varies his accounts of Dora's behavior. Philip's "imperious words" induce her to see Freud.[20]

1901 Freud claims to have written up the Dora case in the two weeks "immediately" following its termination (13n); actually, as his letter to Fliess indicates (1985, 433), he finishes the write-up on January 24.

After the treatment is over, Philip visits Freud a few times (109). In May, Clara, one of the Zellenka children, dies; during a visit to the mourning parents, Dora persuades Hans to admit to the lake-scene overtures and his wife to admit to her love affair with Philip. In October, Dora has an attack of aphonia lasting six weeks, caused by seeing Hans knocked down by a carriage.

1902 In March, Freud's professorship is announced in the newspaper (122n), as a very minor note on the front page of the *Neue Freie Presse*. Two weeks later, afflicted by a facial neuralgia, Dora consults Freud. Upon glancing on her face, Freud judges that she is insincere in seeking therapy.

1903 Dora marries Ernst Adler on December 6.

1905 Dora's only child, a son, is born in April. Dora, her husband, and her son are baptized into the Protestant faith.

1912 Käthe dies.

19. Decker, 1991, 37, 46, 48, 50.
20. *Machtwort*, translated in *S.E.* simply as "authority," 22/180.

1913 Philip dies.

1923 Dora, her husband, and her physician visit Freud. Summoned by Dora's physician, Felix Deutsch visits the bedridden patient in her home.

1932 Ernst, Dora's husband, dies.

1938 Otto, Dora's brother, dies.[21]

1945 Dora dies.

---

21. This great figure of international socialism was given a state funeral attended by such dignitaries as Léon Blum and Friedrich Adler (see Loewenberg, 1984, 188).

2

Bisexuality and Transference

I do not know what kind of help she wanted from me.

Bisexuality constituted a major stumbling block in Freud's treatment of Dora. To understand the nature of that block we must put Dora aside for a while and consider Freud's greatest intimacy with a male in his adult life, a subject that I have explored elsewhere at length (1979). Just a few months before he began Dora's treatment, Freud had what turned out to be his very last meeting with Fliess. The meeting at Achensee also turned out to be a climax in their personal and theoretical entanglement over bisexuality.

Fliess's presence and the issue of bisexuality haunted Freud after their rupture. In 1910 Freud's conflictual attachment to his former confidant still had traumatic repercussions. Thus, when Ferenczi clamored for some semblance of a Fliessian relationship with Freud, the latter replied: "Not only have you noticed that I no *longer* have any need for that full opening of my personality, but you have also understood it and correctly returned to its traumatic cause. Why did you thus make a point of it? This need has been extinguished in me since Fliess's case, with the overcoming of which you saw me occupied. A piece of homosexual investment has been withdrawn and utilized for the enlargement of my own ego" (Freud, 1993b, 221). Contrary to his claim, however, Freud's struggle had not finished, for two months later he announced, as if for the first time, "I have now overcome Fliess, which you were so curious about" (Freud, 1993b, 243).

In fact, Freud never fully came to terms with his relationship with Fliess. When, at the end of 1936, Marie Bonaparte wrote Freud to say that she was about to purchase his as-yet-unpublished letters to Fliess from a bookseller, he responded with shock and hastened to say that he did not want posterity to know about the letters—they were a record of his self-analysis and his amity with Fliess. I was able to discover (Mahony, 1989) that Freud, still shaken some three weeks later, sat down to write "Analysis Terminable and Interminable," an autobiographical treatise that referred to his own interminable self-analysis and the bedrock of sexuality beneath his theoretical quarry. The dead Fliess remained —out of sight, in mind.

By observing the trajectory of Freud's conflicts we can better appreciate their emergence in earlier days. Back in 1896, when Fliess was stressing the theoretical significance of bisexuality, Freud regarded it as the greatest advance in his ongoing research on sexuality, after the concept of defense. Being admittedly "in part neurotic," however, Freud felt disinclined to accept fully Fliess's assumption of bisexuality in everyone. The disinclination seemed to subside, for by December 1896 Freud was writing, "I avail myself of the bisexuality of all human beings." Still, universal bisexuality had to be reclaimed from the waves of internal resistance. The following December, at their meeting in Breslau, with regard to Fliess's position that neuroses are based on the conflict over bisexuality in everyone, Freud uttered: "I've not accepted that yet; I'm not inclined to go into the question" (Freud, 1985, 212, 46, 448; Freud, 1901, 144).

Sometime in the next year Freud became excited about bisexuality, as if seizing on the elusive idea for the first time: "But bisexuality! You are certainly right about it. I am accustoming myself to regarding every sexual act as a process in which four individuals are involved." Not long thereafter, Freud drifted toward the ideology of a masculine monopoly in the psychosexual realm—anxiety, the libido, and even lesbianism were masculine: "What would you say if masturbation were to reduce itself to homosexuality, and the latter, that is, male homosexuality (in both sexes), were the primitive form of sexual longing? (The first

24   BISEXUALITY AND TRANSFERENCE

sexual aim, analogous to the infantile one—a wish that does not
extend beyond the inner world.) If, moreover, libido and anxiety
both were male?" In brief, Freud showed his personal embroilment as he came back to the theory of bisexuality for the nth time
and shuttled between rejecting, modifying, expanding, accepting,
and even forgetting it. His repression of the origin of the theory
even enacted the contribution of bisexuality to repression (Freud,
1985, 292, 364, 380).

Freud's continuing frustration in his clinical practice fueled
his bisexual conflict. In the Dora case itself, the odd account of his
clinical experience with homosexual currents gives the impression of a considerably successful practice; for example, Freud
readily admits that before he learned the importance of homosexuality in neurotics, his cases were often brought to a standstill or
impeded by his perplexity. We know, however, that his clinical
acceptance of bisexuality was quite shaky and not founded on
ample material. In the case history, Freud adds: "I have never yet
come through [durchgekommen] a single psychoanalysis of a man
or a woman without having to take into account a very considerable current of homosexuality" (60/221). The verb durchkommen
can mean "to get through" and even "to succeed." But contrary to
common assumption, Freud did not finish his first psychoanalytic
case until April 1900! That initial success, the case of Mr. E., was
followed by two others that terminated in May; the sexual secrets of these first three were opened by Freud's "keys." From the
start of his systematic self-analysis in mid-1897 until the century
had ended, then, he did not bring any analysis to a successful
conclusion.[1]

The clinical successes of April and May 1900 join with a story
of another order. In a letter to Fliess in May, Freud hedged about
his feminine nature: "But no one can replace for me the relationship with the friend which a special—*possibly* feminine—side
demands" (my italics). Three months later, when the troublesome

1. This circumstance about the talking cure, as I have shown (1994), magni-
fied the importance of the writing cure, whereby Freud conducted his self-analysis. See also Freud, 1985, 409, 413–415.

pair met at Achensee for what proved to be the final turning point in their relationship, Freud propounded the theory of bisexuality as if it were his own idea and an original one at that. Thinking back on the occasion, during which Fliess made a counterclaim of priority, Freud confessed: "I could not recall any such conversation [at Breslau] or this pronouncement of my friend's. One of us must have been mistaken and on the *cui prodest?* principle, it must have been myself. Indeed, in the course of the next week I remembered the whole incident, which was just as my friend had tried to recall it to me" (Freud, 1901, 144).

The following month Freud confessed to Fliess: "I *must* after all take an interest in *reality* in sexuality [read: "bisexuality"], which one learns about only with great difficulty."[2] Freud's struggle with bisexuality and the related conflict over scientific priority clearly involved paternal strivings mobilized in an attempt to ward off a sexually ambivalent submission. He did not know, however, that he was setting the stage for a perturbing clinical encounter.

We have now arrived at the point of being able to make the Viennese connection. Though personally unacquainted, Dora and Fliess both found themselves dealing with Freud's repressed homosexuality and feminine identification. His scriptive addendum about Dora's deepest same-sex strivings toward Peppina links with his guarded reference to the case in a letter to Fliess. Freud did not credit Fliess for the discovery of bisexuality but contented himself to mention his friend's nasal treatment for gastralgia brought about by masturbation (a hint that Fliess could cure some of Dora's troubles by an application of cocaine!). There was also a cloaked reference to Fliess as being uniquely privy to Dora's identity. Then again, we have good grounds to believe that Freud had his epistolary exchanges with Fliess in mind when, commenting on Dora's correspondence with Hans, he said, "Writing gained in importance, as being the only means of communication with him in his absence" (40). Freud, moreover, wrote up his

2. Compare the letters in Freud, 1985, on 412 and 425.

case history for Fliess, whom he imagined as his favorite, best, and prized audience. On another score, Freud thought that blinding jealousy inhabited both Dora and Fliess's wife, both of whom had Ida as a first name.[3]

During the historical month of October 1900, both Dora and Hermann Swoboda, "a severely ill patient," began their analyses with Freud. In the same month Freud told Swoboda of the importance of bisexuality and at one point specified that the human being is "now incubus, now succubus vis-à-vis events, a double attitude explainable in the light of bisexuality itself." In fact, as Freud later reflected, the matter of bisexuality constituted "a substantial part" of the treatment (Freud, 1960, 356).

During that month another patient, a Ms. L.G., was continuing her analysis. She fascinated Freud, who kept a diary on her and, as early as the previous March, made a specific note of her being "at a deeper level gynecophilic" (Freud, 1985, 406). (Her treatment ended in 1901.) The fresh data that I have adduced lead to an assured conclusion. Although Freud's bisexual theory contributed to his first successes six months before seeing Dora and although he was clinically preoccupied with bisexuality in at least two other cases during October, he was not at home with the concept and made restricted use of his hard-won enlightenment.[4]

During Dora's treatment Freud did not address the issue of her homosexuality. His conflicts about it emerge in his postclinical write-up about Dora's bisexuality as introducing a "further complication" that effaces her "poetic" conflict. In other words, whereas Dora's love of a woman obliterates poeticality, her painful involvement with men, as well as Freud's scientific treatment of her involvement, merit the qualification "poetic." The whole subject plunges Freud into rhetorical sleight of hand and some clever fictional writing:

3. Freud, 1985, 374, 456. For Freud's opinion of Ida Fliess, see 196–197n, 447.
4. Freud, 1985, 388, 406, 464, 468; Eissler, 1971, 168; Freud, 1960, 356; Mahony, 1979, 83; Le Rider, 1982, 21, 89. To follow this patient in the Freud-Fliess letters, consult the index of the German edition (Freud, 1986, 606); she is not included in Masson's index to the English edition (Freud, 1985).

I must now turn to consider a further complication to which I should certainly give no space if I were a man of letters engaged upon the creation of a mental state like this for a short story, instead of being a medical man engaged upon its dissection. The element to which I must now allude can only serve to obscure and efface the outlines of the fine poetic conflict which we have been able to ascribe to Dora. This element would rightly fall a sacrifice to the censorship of a writer, for he, after all, simplifies and abstracts when he appears in the character of a psychologist. (59–60)

But no sooner does Freud broach Dora's bisexuality than he generalizes, initially subjugating female sexuality to a male lexicon: "These *masculine or, more properly speaking, gynaecophilic* currents of feeling are to be regarded as typical of the unconscious life of hysterical girls" (63, my italics).

An insight into Freud's own bisexual conflicts turns up unexpectedly in his analysis of Dora's symptomatology. Her coughing had begun as a real irritation, then acted like a grain of sand creating a pearl in the oyster. Thereupon Dora's symptom expressed both sympathetic identification with her tubercular father and regret during Hans's absences. After reflecting further on the symptom, Freud states that a girl wanting to replace her oedipal mother may develop the same painful symptom as her mother; but the girl—and here Freud uses Dora as an example—may also identify with her coughing father as an oedipal expression of love for him. In the latter case, object-choice regresses to identification (1921, 106–107).

Later, Dora's symptom representing coitus with her father was based on an identification with Peppina (47–48, 51, 56, 83). According to Freud's reconstruction, Dora's primary erotogenic zone was the mucous membrane of the lips and mouth and was marked by a subsequent somatic compliance: she sucked the breast, then a thumb, and then, in fantasy, the penis. Dora's coughing and throat irritation proclaimed an unconscious orogenital fantasy in which Peppina sucked Philip's penis: "But the conclusion was inevitable that with her spasmodic cough, which, as is usual, was referred for its exciting stimulus to a tickling in her throat, she pictured to herself a scene of sexual gratification *per os* between the two people whose love affair occupied her mind so incessantly" (48).

It is to Lacan's credit (1951) that he was the very first to criticize specifically Freud's male bias in his heterosexual interpretation of Dora's symptom. According to Freud, Dora's thumb-sucking up to the age of five furnished "the necessary somatic prerequisite" for a fantasy, represented by her cough, of fellatio between her reportedly impotent father and Peppina. To this reconstruction Lacan objects: "One is surprised here that Freud does not see that the aphonia brought on during the absences of Herr K. expresses the violent call of the oral erotic drive when Dora was 'one on one' with Frau K., without there being any need for him to invoke her awareness of the *fellatio* undergone by the father, when everyone knows that *cunnilingus* is the artifice most commonly adopted by 'men of means' whose powers begin to abandon them" (221, my translation). Freud, in his manhandling of Dora, eschewed cunnilingus for fellatio and offered an orogenital interpretation whose patriarchal taxonomy was embedded not in a gynecophilology but in a gynecophobology.

In spite of Lacan's correction, let us not forget that Dora merely referred to gratification *per os* but did not specify who was doing what to whom. I further suggest the possibility that Dora's symptom translated a gynecophilic orogenital component. It is quite to the point that the German for Dora's throat itch or tickling is *Kitzel*, a cognate of *Kitzler* (207/48), the German for "clitoris." Over time Dora's coughing would have appeared to acquire the meaning of cunnilingus with Peppina. In effect, the tickling or itching constituted a symptom with an accumulative symbolism: if it began as an identification with her tubercular father, it eventually could have denoted a repressed fantasy of her cunnilingus with Peppina. Within this context Freud's misunderstanding of Dora's cough—a derivative of his homosexual conflicts with Fliess—doubly denies a woman's same-sex orogenital love: he replaces it with a heterosexual scene of the woman giving pleasure to the man. Echoing in the background is a statement made by Freud not long before the Dora case; he wondered whether male homosexuality represents "the primitive form of sexual longing" in both sexes (in Freud's patriarchal expansiveness, even in her love for another of her sex, a woman is a man possessed— Freud, 1985, 380).

Another aspect of thematic bisexuality becomes evident when we consider it from an editorial perspective, beginning with *The Interpretation of Dreams* and turning to the Dora case and *Three Essays on the Theory of Sexuality* (1905b). The Dreambook unfolds as the male author's oedipal and then preoedipal exploration of the mother's body (Mahony, 1987). But during the composition of the book Freud as author has a female identification: the book is his "child of sorrow" and "dream-child." The censor, castrator, even "godfather" of that book was Fliess. The bisexual conflicts between the two men contributed to the prolonged gestation of the book and its delayed publication. With hindsight (polysemy intended) we can speak of Freud's overdetermined anal retentiveness with respect to his creation, which he called his "dung heap."[5]

Soon after the publication of the Dreambook, on November 4, 1900, Freud declared that the full parturition of his theoretical psychosexuality was delayed: "With regard to the sexual theory, I still want to wait. An unborn piece remains attached to what has already been born" (Freud, 1985, 387). The subject of that unborn piece was Dora, whose continual frustration of Freud, culminating in her abrupt termination of treatment, compounded his castration and the feminine identity that surged in his tumultuous relationship with Fliess. Because the clinical absence of bisexuality from Dora's therapy points to the repressed presence of Fliess, the scriptive emergence of the theme in the case history takes on a multisided significance.

Freud's understanding of bisexuality underwent two phases

5. Freud, 1985, 353, 359, 405, 412; compare letter of September 6, 1899 (370).

during his write-up of the Dora case. In Phase 1, Freud wrote his first draft, where he dealt sparingly and uneasily with bisexuality. In the final pages of chapter 1, Freud speaks of Dora's love for Peppina as typifying the unconscious homosexual feelings of hysterical girls.[6] The day after finishing his composition, Freud wrote to Fliess that the Dora case contains "glimpses of the sexual-organic foundation" of hysteria, but he said nothing of bisexuality; nor did he tell his "first audience" that his discovery had occurred only during the write-up (Freud, 1985, 433). In his next letter, dated January 30, in what appears to be a response to Fliess's offended reaction, Freud added that the case helped him realize once and for all that "the principal issue in the conflicting thought processes is the contrast between an inclination toward men and an inclination toward women" (Freud, 1985, 434; see the editorial comment in Freud, 1986, n. 2).

In Phase 2, sometime between the end of January 1901, when the case was written up, and 1905, when it was published, Freud came to attribute his technical failure to Dora's bisexuality. He says in a footnote to the "Postscript": "The longer the interval of time that separates me from the end of this analysis, the more probable it seems to me that the fault in my technique lay in this omission: I failed to discover in time and to inform Dora of her homosexual [gynecophilic] love" (120).[7] Freud's technical failure with Dora's bisexuality was bound up with his conflicts over precipitancy and waiting: rushing to publish the case but postponing a full treatment of bisexuality. That dilatoriness, the very action he accuses Dora of, persisted while he was working on

6. In this portion of the text, we can perceive a meaningful unsteadiness in Freud's expository tone. Roof (1991, 187) acutely observes that Dora's gynecophilic strivings "are abundantly and redundantly characterized, occurring three times in an uncannily similar phraseology, twice within two pages." Both Roof and Jacobus (1986) call attention to Freud's terminological slippage, as on several occasions he assimilates the woman's same-sex love into a male-oriented designation (see also Jacobus, 1986, 120n).

7. The rest of that sequential footnote, tying in the second dream, Dora's bisexuality, and Peppina as the source of Dora's sexual knowledge, complements the end of the footnotes on pages 105 and 110–111. I conjecture that the three passages in question were composed during a later editorial revision.

Three Essays on the Theory of Sexuality, when he labored to "avoid the topic of bisexuality as far as possible" (Freud, 1985, 464). The discussion of Freud's wide-reaching difficulties with bisexuality has touched on transferential issues that must be explored. It is erroneous to think that Freud made his clinical discovery about transference with the Dora case. In *Studies on Hysteria* (1893–1895), Freud was already aware of patients' transference during "cathartic analysis." The transference that Freud pictured at that time, however, was sporadic and localized rather than perduring and pervasive. Being "the worst obstacle that we can come across," the transference, Freud opined, could emerge when the patient felt disfavored, feared losing independence, or made a false connection by "transferring on to the figure of the physician the distressing ideas which arise from the content of the analysis" (301, 302).[8]

Just as Freud's realization of transference in the *Studies on Hysteria* came only after he had finished the early treatments, so Freud's transferential insights in the Dora case occurred after its termination. The story of transference in the latter instance is one of both greater darkness and greater light. Given Freud's profound new understanding of clinical transference (*Übertragung*) in the case history, it behooves us to realize that he was preoccupied with the term in other senses. In the case history, Freud uses *übertragen(e),* the past participle of *übertragen* (to transfer), three times to mean transmitting physical illness and once to indicate a transference of disgust (237–238/75, 247/84). The translations in the *Standard Edition* are, respectively, "handed on," "handed on," "handed . . . on," and "transferred." Did the term *Übertragung* facilitate Freud's belated awareness of transference or delay it? We do not know, but we may advance an explanation and, in doing so, coin a critical term: *Übertragung* was a linguistic activator that

8. Freud, 1893–1895, 301, 302. Clearly, then, as early as 1895 Freud recognized the importance, albeit negative, of transference in the therapeutic process. Strachey erroneously claims that in the Dora case Freud indicates for the first time "the importance of transference as a factor in the therapeutic process of psychoanalysis" (118n).

could have preconsciously stirred up Freud's alertness to its multiple implications.

Freud went beyond his position in *Studies on Hysteria* that transference is the greatest technical obstacle to realizing its potential as the most powerful ally in analysis. He also managed to detect two kinds of transference: some transferences are merely new reprints that differ in no way from their past prototypes, and others are revised editions.[9] Nevertheless, Freud continued to think of transference as a partial rather than a global phenomenon: "Owing to the readiness with which Dora put one part of the pathogenic material at my disposal during the treatment, I *forgot* the precaution of looking out for *the first signs of transference, which was being prepared in connection with another part of the material—a part of which I was in ignorance*" (118, my italics). This passage is taken from the *Standard Edition,* except that I have substituted "forgot" for Strachey's mistranslation of *vergass* as "neglected." The faulty rendering leaves open the possibility that Freud was aware of, yet unwilling to apply, his conscious knowledge. Freud plainly says, however, that he forgot to look for the first signs of transference. Then, as if forgetting what he had just announced, Freud proceeded on the same page to declare that at the outset Dora had been explicitly associating him with her suspect father!

Further indicative of Freud's personal turmoil was his assertion that during his treatment, transference "never came into question with the patient"—a generalized claim that he contradicts twice. Freud pointed out that Dora's first or fire dream had an allusion to himself as a smoker (he kept to himself, however, that she also wanted a kiss from him). Yet while examining the dream, Freud came close to an engaging transference interpretation. Significantly, he relegated that interpretation to a footnote in his write-up, its typographic position signaling its subordinate con-

9. It is interesting to watch Freud juggling with this double division in his later essay on technique "Observations on Transference-Love" (1915). In the first two-thirds of the essay Freud maintains that transference love is merely a reprint, with "not a single new element"; then, in a turnabout, he concludes that transference love disregards reality "to a high [but not complete] degree."

tent: "You are summoning up your old love for your father in order to protect yourself against your love for Herr K. . . . *The reappearance of the dream in the last few days forces me to the conclusion that you consider the same situation has arisen once again, and that you have decided to give up the treatment*—to which, after all, it is only your father who makes you come. . . . The sequel showed how correct my guess had been. *At this point my interpretation touches for a moment upon the subject of transference"* (70 and n., my italics).[10]

The italicized statements should not be overread. Freud himself thought that his interpretation had but brushed against (*streift*) the transference (232n/70n). In a belated gesture of self-supervision, he provided the transferential interpretation that he should have made: "But when the first dream came, in which she gave herself the warning that she had better leave my treatment just as she had formerly left Herr K.'s house, I ought to have listened to the warning myself. 'Now,' I ought to have said to her, 'it is from Herr K. that you have made a transference on to me. Have you noticed anything that leads you to suspect me of evil intentions similar (whether openly or in some sublimated form) to Herr K.'s? Or have you been struck by anything about me or got to know anything about me which has caught your fancy, as happened previously with Herr K.?' " (118).

The fragility of Freud's transferential awareness was revealed again when, several weeks later, he had so repressed his interpretation that he was completely surprised by Dora's announcement that she was leaving treatment (105). Truly, Freud repressed some of the insights into transference that he had revealed at the end of *Studies on Hysteria*. What are we to conclude from the absence of transferential interpretation from the Dora case (except

10. This practice resembles Freud's defensive use of footnotes elsewhere as a typographical demotion of what could risk being highlighted in his main text, such as the all-critical assumption that the Rat Man masturbated in childhood (1909, 206–208n) or the avowal in the Wolf Man case of his greatest clinical doubt (1918, 103n). Compare van den Berg's (1987, 62) lapidary remark: "Perhaps footnotes, too, are a kind of resistance."

in two passages relating to the first dream)? Did Freud merely use an outdated therapeutic technique?

Insofar as transferential interpretation is a sine qua non of psychoanalytic treatment, the habitual classification of the Dora case as a psychoanalytic treatment is an instance of misnomer. Analysts have traditionally included the case within the great clinical classics of psychoanalytic treatment (Mahony, 1993a). That is wrong.

Let us now examine Dora's transferential reaction to Freud and its immediate determinants. Before she began her treatment with Freud, she was in the throes of traumatic reactions that compounded her distressful adolescent development. Only close attention to textual nuances enables us to understand the full import of Dora's fainting. The "first" fainting attack, which occurred during an argument with Philip, sometime after her half-hearted suicidal threat, was decisive in his bringing her to Freud. Nevertheless, more fainting fits occurred before her treatment, including the "last" one, when Dora, expressing her hatred of the Zellenkas, demanded that her father break with them (23, 26, 42). The picture emerging prior to treatment is that of an adolescent in a crescendo of turmoil; the rage that she had toward her entourage was redirected onto herself in a psychosomatic symptom. Still living at home and immaturely immersed in her parents, hampered by psychosomatic symptoms persisting for an unfair share of life, entrapped in a romantic machination, and bounded by self-serving adults, Dora received no real solace in reaching down the sorrowful corridors of her memory.

Into Freud's waiting room she stepped, author of a recent suicide note, victim of fainting spells with possible convulsions, putative confabulator for about two and a half years, and distraught adolescent nearing her eighteenth birthday. However much Dora had fought off the recklessness of familial collusion, she now found herself in the office of another doctor, the same one who knew Hans and who had treated her father and her aunt. Her father had recently seen Freud several times (26). In the light of Dora's panicky state and deep sense of betrayal by men, I doubt that she lay on Freud's couch at the start of therapy. The famous photos of that couch with its billowy pillows give the impression that his patients leaned back rather than lay on it; such large pillows, moreover, would obstruct Freud's view if he was sitting directly behind it. At one point, however, we do read about Dora's lying on the couch and Freud's observing her as she fingered her purse (76).[11] Had he changed his position, or were the large cushions removed? Once the treatment was under way, Dora and Freud found themselves at loggerheads. In spite of her "intellectual precocity," her "critical powers" and "high level" of intellectual upbringing (88), his dislike of Dora reinforced his patriarchal phallic prejudice. Eroticizing the case from the very beginning as a contribution to his self-styled "picklocks" for hysteria, Freud required Dora to play a minor service role for his theories (Freud, 1985, 427).

Together with his self-concerned and authoritarian needs, Freud's scientific intentions prevented him from freely listening and experiencing surprise, as he recognized subsequently: "Cases which are devoted from the first to scientific purposes and are treated accordingly suffer in their outcome; while the most successful cases are those in which one proceeds, as it were, without any purpose in view, allows oneself to be taken by surprise by any new turn in them, and always meets them with an open mind, free from any presuppositions" (1912, 114). To shore up his scientific procedure, Freud used neutral language in discussing sexuality. He said that he did not hesitate to discuss sexuality frankly with "a young female *person*" (*einer jugendlichen weiblichen Person*).[12] If Dora's mother, Käthe, was an obsessional Hausfrau, Freud tried to

---

11. I would like to know more about the early staging of Dora's dramatic self-presentation and Freud's perception of it. On the impact of the relations of power and representation in the social system on hysteria in the nineteenth century, the interaction of hysteria and the invention of photography, and the cross-referenced manifestations of hysteria in Charcot's dramatic and pictorial demonstrations of his scientific knowledge, see Didi-Huberman, 1982.

12. The translation in *S.E.*, "a young woman" (165/9), eliminates Freud's defensive and not so redundant "person."

be a kind of scrupulous Wortfrau, bent on the use of "dry and direct" words with Dora—dry goods.[13]

Another matter is Dora's enormous strain, which would be amplified after her initial encounter with Freud. During the treatment, Dora manifested no noticeable improvement apart from the cessation of coughing (48), but we are not told whether she had any bouts of fainting. Freud also refers to her fainting fits as attacks, *Anfälle* (compare 181n/23n and 202/42), and we do read that after treatment, her "attacks" became less frequent (115, 121). Is Freud implying that Dora was fainting throughout her treatment? And what about other symptoms? Freud's concluding assertion that during psychoanalytic treatment old symptoms do not disappear nor do new symptoms form (115, 116) undercuts his earlier report. For whatever reason, Dora's cough did disappear after an interpretation (48); and "a professedly new symptom, which consisted of piercing gastric pain," appeared.

Dora's compliance gives rise to many questions. Did Dora tell Freud as much as she did because she trusted him or because she relented to his pressure? Was supplying Freud with sexual material in part a seductive compliance, her jewelry gift to him, much like the jewelry gifts that Philip showered on Peppina? If so, that compliance was in turn undercut by her repeated resistance and her frequent amnesia, as when she did not remember whether she loved her father intensely. Then again, did she resist Freud by feeding into his interpretations with stimulating morsels so that he could be further seduced and she could further resist him?

13. In the patriarchal context of sexual exchange, where women are chattel, Freud strives in his own way for a corrective discourse. In the insightful words of Sprengnether (1990, 48): If we bear in mind Freud's interpretive tactics of turning no into yes and of seeing Dora's accusations as self-reproaches, then "one may interpret Freud's furious denial of the charge of titillating his patient with sexual language, coupled with his anxiety about being so reproached, as an indication that he is doing just that." There may be, however, a return of the libidinally repressed when Freud couches his feline boasting in French: "J'appelle un chat un chat" (48). Decker (1991, 119) glosses Freud's directness with the linguistic note that in German *Kätzchen* means "kitten" as well as "pussy," or "female genitalia." In addition, let me point out the homophony of *chat, Katharina,* and *catarrh* (*Katarrh*), Dora's name for her vaginal infection.

When she said that she could think of nothing else but the relationship between her father and Peppina, how much of that was a transferential defense? A partial answer is that her ambivalence led her to rebel, in her own way forcing Freud in male genderlect to conclude, "I get nothing out of her."[14]

The therapeutic process of the dyad stumbled when it involved the Zellenkas, Dora criticizing everyone except Peppina, and Freud criticizing all the adults except Hans. Fliess also figured in the manifold interaction between Freud and Dora. As we know, Freud and Fliess increasingly rejected each other's theories toward the end of their relationship; Freud indicted the numerologist, and Fliess the "thoughts-reader" (Freud, 1985, 440). In reacting to Dora, Freud became a caricature of the thoughts-reader, fulfilling Fliess's accusation with a vengeance. Like Fliess but in her own parlance, Dora accused Freud of mind reading. And he thought that she had paranoid traits, a negativity that he later saw in Fliess.

As could be expected, the theme of knowledge and secrets—so charged in any patriarchal context of power—takes up a salient place in the Dora case. especially in that Freud linked Dora's source of knowledge with her lesbian strivings (120n). A whirligig of motives affected Freud's stance. Guided by his tenet that a hysterical symptom and sexual ignorance cannot happen together, he proceeded with delicate caution not to "contaminate" Dora with physiological knowledge. His delicacy, we must remark, came not from tenderness for Dora but rather from a desire for scientific purity. Freud forswore any possibility of deriving

14. A considerable amount of work remains to be done on the synergy between male genderlect and the dreams from which psychoanalysis arose. I have demonstrated (1986), for example, that in the only piece of dialogue in the Irma dream, both Freud and Irma begin their utterances with "if," a lexical repetition suggesting an apparent identification between the two speakers. But paradoxically, the repetition is nonidentical: Freud's pseudo-suppositional "if" really means "given the fact that," whereas Irma's "if" followed by the subjunctive indicates an unfulfilled desire. In his chauvinistic dream Freud as the male medical authority speaks facts, is accusatory, and uses a logical syntax of antecedence and consequence; the female patient utters hopeless desire, is defensive, and uses broken syntax.

pleasure from sexual exchanges with Dora: "I took the greatest pains with this patient not to introduce her to *any fresh facts in the region of sexual knowledge*; and I did this, not from any conscientious motives, but because I was anxious to subject my assumptions to a rigorous test" (31, my italics). Freud uncovered a number of possible sources for Dora's existing sexual knowledge: the male-governed written tradition of books and encyclopedias and the female oral tradition—Dora's governess, her cousin, and Peppina (36, 61, 111n).[15] But he was also grew frustrated, as we realize by comparing two comments. Very early on, he says that whereas her answers about the content of her sexual knowledge were quick and frank, her memories did not solve the riddle of its source. By the end of the case, we read that she was "always pretending not to know where her knowledge came from" (compare 31, 120n).

In pursuit of answers, Freud fastened on the need to find out where she had learned about penile erection and fellatio—only to conclude that a fantasy of fellatio does not necessarily mean that enlightenment was received from external sources (31, 47, 51). But Freud did not remain content with endopsychic answers. In mutually glossing passages, he railed at Dora's "pitiless" perception and memory of her father's philanderings and her contrasting inability to recall where she had found out about an erection (31, 32). Who was ignoring, who ignorant? Chased by Hans, chastened by Freud, Dora had much to learn.

Ironically, Freud's struggle for knowledge thrusts him into an unwelcome resemblance to Dora. On one hand, we see Freud the therapist bitingly accusing Dora of withholding the fount of her sexual enlightenment (he did not realize then that her repeated denials about her knowledge and experience might well have been a post-traumatic reaction of identifying with the adult ag-

15. Compare Jacobus (1986, 188): "At once the hole through which sexual, social and economic oppression leaks into the family and the source of contaminating knowledge, the governess proves in the last resort to be only ambiguously differentiated from Dora or Frau K., or even from Dora's mother (whose role is that of a domestic)."

gressors around her). On the other hand, we see Freud the author feeling reproachful, complaining that whereas previously he had been accused of giving conclusions without supplying sources, now he expected accusations for being indiscreet by identifying sources of the information.

Dora's concern was historical truth; Freud's was psychic genetic truth. The temporal focus of Freud's interpretive concerns was the internal, not the external; and even then he examined not the transference but rather Dora's continued love for Hans. Following up Erik Erikson's reservations (1964), specialists in adolescent development have indicated further problems in the case: Freud's countertransference with both his own and Dora's adolescence; his neglect of Dora's age-appropriate idealism and search for validation of her experience; and his insensitivity to her adolescent conflict over wishing to be both independent and dependent. His attitude resembled that of nineteenth-century parents, who hardly recognized the independent identities of their adolescent children. From another quarter came this tried and true counsel: "As we consider Dora's disruption of her analysis in developmental terms, we could say, today, that the consolidation of her neurotic condition had been short-circuited by the fact that her analysis was being conducted as if an adult neurosis already existed. As a consequence, the adolescent ego became overwhelmed by interpretations it was unable to integrate, and it simply took to flight. If there is one thing adolescent analysis has taught us, it is that ill-timed id interpretations are unconsciously experienced by the adolescent as a parental—that is, incestuous —seduction."[16] Freud's quest for his own version of truth thus made it difficult for Dora to differentiate him from her father and Hans.

Sometimes Freud comes across less like a therapist than like an exasperated parent with a rebellious teenager. But his ignoring of Dora's adolescence does not excuse his bad technique. He did

16. Blos, 1972, 130. See also Erikson, 1964, 171, 172, 174; Scharfman, 1980, 50–51; Kanzer, 1980, 75, 79; and Sand, 1983, 350.

not like her, period. Instead of working with and building on Dora's idealism, he badgered her. She became the scapegoat of Freud's loathing for the hypocritical society ladies of Vienna depicted in the Katharina case, or so I assume (1989). We could go through the case to note the drumroll of Freud's aggression toward Dora, starting with his flipping her reproaches back at her and turning her nos into yeses. He complained about her "incessant repetition" and "usual contradictions" (54, 108). Before, she was caught in the network of family machinations; now, in addition, she was caught in the ever-tightening network of explanations that Freud imposed. When she lamented her gastric pains, Freud asked, "Whom are you copying now?" and reflected in a triumphant tone that he "had hit the mark" (38). On another page Freud informs us about learning a fact that he "did not fail to use against her" (59). He also told her that he hoped her father would not be convinced that she was ill, for then it would become a powerful weapon that she would always use to get her way.[17] He nowhere suggests that she might have been identifying with adult malingerers.

Freud got as far as interpreting Dora's oedipal attachment to her father, but overreaction to her resistance made him overlook the negative transference in various materials that she brought. Was Freud like her father, who thought of his own enjoyment and saw things to suit himself? Was her early memory about sucking her thumb and tugging Otto's ear as he sat quietly beside her a transferential allusion to trying to gain a paternal ear? Freud passed over Dora's governess, who pretended interest in her but was really interested in her father; might this have been a transferential reference to Dora's perception of Freud? Even at the end, when Freud finally retrospected about Dora's transferential ven-

17. Although we hear from Freud that Dora laughed at her former physicians for their ineffectiveness, we do not hear how painful her electrical and hydropathic treatments were. After years of ineffectual treatment, Dora might have reacted with more independence than scorn (Decker, 1991). Freud never mentioned the pain of such procedures, although he later did during his official pronouncements about the electrical treatment used for war neuroses (Eissler, 1986, 26, 69, 72); this omission is revelatory of his negative countertransference in the Dora case.

geance, he did not perceive at least some of it as a retort to his own abuse of her, which continued the abuse of other males in her life. Paternalism on all fours.

We must bring both Freud's hostility and his neglect of the transference to bear on his belief that it is "only after the transference has been resolved that a patient arrives at a sense of conviction of the validity of the connections which have been constructed during the analysis" (116–117). If we take Freud at his word, it follows that Dora could *not* have been convinced by his interpretations and constructions. But Freud did not take himself at his own word: neglectful of the transference, he harassed her with interpretations and accused her throughout of resistance. Notwithstanding the absence of transferential interpretation and, a fortiori, resolution of the transference, Freud wanted to hold her responsible for the failure of the treatment. In effect, he often opted for rhetorical rather than psychoanalytic engagement with Dora. He repeatedly set aside interpreting for the sake of arguing, and he argued too soon at that. We recall Freud's much later retrospection: "In former years I often had occasion to find that the premature communication of a solution brought the treatment to an untimely end" (1913, 140–141). His browbeating ministrations were companion to his impatience with working through, and his intrusive couchside manner attended an impetuous desire to impress and overcome his charge with the display of bedeviling associations. Dora was caught between two forces: her gastric symptoms, which called or spoke out (*sagten . . . aus*, 197/38; *rief . . . hinaus*, 245/82),[18] and Freud as her spokesperson (*Fürsprecher*), who inferred her unconscious thoughts and put them into first-person expressions for her (for example, 82, 85).

Freud endorsed Philip's romantic scheme of giving Dora to Hans and would hence appear as another in the circle of adults

18. Elsewhere Freud names this phenomenon *mitsprechen*: *G.W* 1:398/*S.E.*, 3:180; *G.W.*, 1:212, 301/*S.E.*, 2:148, 296; *G.W.*, 12:107/*S.E.*, 17:76. In short, being dispossessed of her voice was manifest in Dora's symptoms, fantasies, object relations, and indeed in her whole identity.

who pretended an interest in Dora but who at any moment of frustration would turn against her. "She was a source of heavy trials for her parents" (23), we read. But the sources of her troubles were multiple, starting with traumas and proceeding to Freud's trial of her. Far from a sustaining protection, Freud's treatment of Dora, his attempted indoctrination of her to be the sacrificial lamb, amounted to iatrogenic trauma: Dora should marry the man who calumniated her, the one who assessed her and the governess as sexually disposable objects. Dora wanted Freud to validate her perceptions of the erotic machinations of her immediate milieu; this he did. She also wanted him to side with her in opposing her father's liaison; this he did not do. Rather, he tried to show her that she was erotically involved much as the Zellenkas and her father were, and he even tried to have her comply with their scheming by getting married. This she did not do.

Quite unlike his warm grandfatherliness toward little Hans or his fatherliness toward the Rat Man, Freud's attitude in Dora's case was hard and cold. In session after session he subjected her to interpretations of her hostility, and he treated her as a dyed-in-the-wool avenger. Even the possible exception—her mothering of the Zellenka children—he undermined as exploitative. He called Dora's observations pitiless, whereas he expressed pity for the " poor" fired governess who was enamored of Philip and who pretended to befriend Dora. Described as having no salvageable good, healthy identifications in her, she comes across as a vengeful little bitch. As time passed during the treatment and perhaps also during the write-up, Freud became more and more embittered with her, finally ascribing to her a nearly "malignant vindictiveness" (105n).

Until the very end of the treatment Freud tried to lock Dora in his interpretations of a strictly heterosexual dynamic. Retrospecting about Dora, Freud admits: "I do not know what kind of help she wanted from me" (122). Freud's confessed ignorance was influenced by shying away from female transference. He could not see that he resembled the seductive Peppina, with whom Dora discussed sexual topics.

The pseudonym that Freud conferred on Ida Bauer contributed to her physical and social loss of voice. I shall restrict myself to a short discussion of this much-discussed topic. In *The Psychopathology of Everyday Life,* Freud relates how he chose an alias for Dora. During a visit with his sister Rosa, he learned that because she and her nursemaid bore the same first name, the latter had been given the name Dora. Thus, Freud reflected, poor people "cannot even keep their own names" (1901, 241). And so, as he was penning his case history, only the name Dora came to him: "The complete absence of alternatives was here based on a solid association connected with the subject-matter that I was dealing with: for it was a person employed in someone else's house, a governess, who exercised a decisive influence on my patient's story, and on the course of the treatment as well." Such a naming falls in line with his feeling that she acted like a maid. Thus, upon learning from Dora that she was terminating treatment at the end of the session and that she had arrived at the decision two weeks previously, Freud remarked: "That sounds just like a maidservant or a governess—a fortnight's warning" (105).[19] We must also bear in mind that when Freud went to the same Dresden museum as Dora did, for him Raphael's Madonna resembled a nursemaid (1960, 97).[20]

Throughout the heterosexual script in the Dora case and other major case histories, all warped by his patriarchal assumptions, Freud downplayed the mother.[21] A product of the cobbling-

19. Compare Gearhart, 1979, 124, and Gallop, 1982, 141–142.
20. Marcus (1975) traced Dora to her incompetent namesake in Dickens's *David Copperfield.* Decker (1991) makes much of the various Doras that Freud registered when watching Victorien Sardou's play *Théodora;* she also (136–137) found extensive resemblances between Freud's protagonist and Breuer's daughter Dora, as well as Freud's famous patient Anna O. Malcolm (1981) links Pandora and Dora's overdetermined use of "box," explained by Freud as also referring to woman and to her genitalia (97). Rogow (1978, 341) suggests that Freud's retaliatory name choice was motivated by anger with Dora for leaving him. Kanzer (1980, 80) maintains an overdetermined coincidence between Freud's four-year delay in publishing his case and the four years' age difference between Freud and his favorite sister, Rosa.
21. In one passage Freud says that despite Dora's depressed condition, she was attending lectures for women and pursuing "more or less serious studies" (*ernstere Studien,* 181/23). The grammatical point here is that a comparative adjec-

together of psychosexual theory and patriarchal ideology, his marital plan for Dora would also have entailed a divorce between the Bauers—that is, would have ousted Käthe from her marriage, much as he excluded her from Dora's case history. Whereas Freud modified, even inverted so many of Dora's reports about others, he did not alter her report that her mother was unlikable. It did not help matters that although Freud saw Philip several times before, during, and after Dora's treatment (109), he never laid eyes on her mother. And, we may wonder, Did he see Hans during that period?

Evidence abounds that Käthe was more present in Dora's psychodynamics than Freud would allow. Dora chose to recount the lake trauma only to her mother, who then told her husband. During a certain period of the treatment Dora identified with her mother in symptom and manner, yet that identification receives but a one-sentence description in Freud's text. In associating to her two dreams Dora made substantial mention of her mother, who is acknowledged but quickly shelved by Freud. Dora's identification with her mother as victimized by a male-transmitted disease also induced her to be that much more distrustful of Freud. Let us note, too, that Dora's persistent identification with her mother emerged clearly in the Deutsch interview years later, when Dora talked about her chronic constipation and her preoccupation with bodily cleanliness.

Most of Dora's defenses were unshaken and perhaps even reinforced by treatment. Although she did not let herself go into a fully regressive maternal transference, there are glimpses of a preoedipal transference in which she sought the idealized phallic mother with whom she had the putative cunnilingual fantasy I mentioned earlier. Although in a fleeting mention Freud did identify Peppina with the vengeful Medea, he omitted to explore the

---

tival form, *ernstere*, for instance, can sometimes be used not in the sense of comparison but in the sense of "rather" or "more or less." Ignoring that usage, Masson (1988, 52) takes Freud to task for holding that Dora's attendance at feminist lectures was trivial in comparison with her "more serious" studying.

split between never hearing Dora criticize Peppina and knowing that many such criticisms were heard by her father (compare 26, 62).[22]

Freud identified with the potent Hans and the sexually frustrated Hans. The object of Freud's hyperidentification, Hans stands as the only major protagonist in the case history whom Freud exempted from criticism. It is not insignificant that, like Fliess, Hans courted a woman named Ida. Freud and Hans became strange bedfellows in their attempts to overpower Dora's (Ida's) resistance, to corner and importune her. Nor is it insignificant that despite Hans's exploitative and mendacious character, Freud was convinced of his serious marital intentions toward Dora two and a half years previously.[23]

Freud also resembled Dora, yet how their identifications interacted and even complemented one another eludes a complete answer. Although he would have argued that his professional discretion differed from her secrecy, in reproaching her he concealed from himself that they shared certain fantasies and defenses. Throughout the case history he does not hesitate to reproach a series of people, including readers past and future, for their contradictory criticisms that he both indiscreetly discloses confidential information and discusses sex frankly with a girl. But he fails to draw the conclusion that his own tit-for-tat principle invites: that in reproaching her, he reproached himself. Even at the end, when he reflects on Dora's transferential vengeance, he cannot see that at least some of it was a response to his own abuse of her, that he himself identified with Dora the aggressor. In their

22. Slipp (1977), Meissner (1984), and various feminist scholars have been sensitive to the idealized omnipotent mother in Dora's psychodynamics. See also Ornstein (1993, 81n): "The discussions of Dora's femininity in the literature assume a much more advanced level of emotional maturity than she was ever capable of attaining. Yes, her femininity was an issue—but still served earlier, more archaic needs."

23. Jacobus (1986, 173) astutely asks what Freud's screened self-reproach would have been if he had identified with Philip or, more self-threateningly, with Dora as the lover of Peppina. Actually, Freud resembles Philip in the use of detours—see the indirection in Freud's reliance on Latin (*per os*, 48) and French (48, 49).

defensive attitude toward one another, each countered the other's ambivalence, with Freud in particular overlooking Dora's attraction to him in her antagonism. They joined in exhibitionism, she displaying her illness, he his phallic interpretive power. Their mutual acting-out and pathogenic interplay subverted the analytic process: Freud's experimental and theoretical zeal relegated the analytic process to second place, and Dora wanted Freud to help end her father's alliance.[24]

If, early on, Freud attributed his main failure in the case to having forgotten the transference, he later thought that he had overlooked Dora's homosexual love for Peppina.[25] In saying that Dora's homosexual love for Peppina was beneath all her displacements (*Verschiebungen*, 267n/105n), Freud was tracing the displacements to a single source. His use of *Verschiebung* here differs from his usage elsewhere, where the term may be translated either as "displacement" (implying that there was a right place to start with) or as "shifting" (having no implication about a right place); sometimes it means "displacement," sometimes "shifting," and at other times, in a postmodern subversion of the idea of origins, it shifts inconclusively between those two meanings. In any event, detailed evidence is lacking as to just how Dora's bisexual and transferential dynamics could have combined into a transference in which Freud was Peppina, Käthe, or both in their own endless identifications. Was Freud so mobilized, so castrated by what he perceived as Dora's vengeance that he warded off his resultant feminization and his therefore homoerotic contact? We might conclude that in treating Dora, Freud once more held at bay his own feminine identification and kept in suspense the en-

24. Compare Ramas, 1980; Gearhart, 1979, 124; Collins et al., 1979, 37–39; and Hertz, 1979, 68–70.

25. Lacan (1951) was the first to highlight Freud's self-avowed wavering over the failure of Dora's treatment as due to his having overlooked transferential and homosexual factors. Lacan also made the interesting observation that by overidentifying with Hans, Freud misinterpreted Dora's responses as agreements. In fact, they were attacks on himself. For an interesting critique of Lacan's elaboration of his main thesis, see Gearhart, 1979. Lacan makes a number of factual errors in reporting the Dora case, just as he does in his article on the Rat Man (Mahony, 1986a).

meshed difficulties with transference and homosexuality that he had with Fliess, the husband of another Ida.

We may also wonder how the class difference increased Freud's distaste for being treated as a transferential same-sex object. Dora treated him like a maid, a fact that Freud blindly turned into its contrary during the treatment. In this regard, the implications of Freud's statements in his introductory chapter have gone completely unnoticed. He wrote up the case "during the two weeks immediately following" termination (13n); his correspondence with Fliess contains explicit references to writing the case history between January 10 and 24, a two-week period, although he may have started it on January 1 (Freud, 1985, 432, 433). At any rate, Freud's statement in the "Prefatory Remarks" shows that he himself identified with a maid, dismissing—writing up—the case within two weeks.

If issues of transference and same-sex love never came together in Freud's understanding during the treatment, neither were they integrated in his write-up. In effect, we are confronted with a double split in his countertransference to bisexuality that alerts us to the intensity of his entangled conflicts. In the opening month of Dora's treatment, Freud was blind to her same-sex strivings but not to those of contemporary patients; neither in his case write-up nor in its "Postscript" did Freud integrate the issues of transference and homosexuality. The text follows clinical progression, but only up to a point; otherwise, it is scrambled. He first reveals Dora's bisexuality midway through the text, although he did not become aware of it until well after the treatment; in the main text of the "Postscript," he discusses transference but not bisexuality.

Let me close with a biblical story (Genesis 32:24–32) whose full relevance to Freud merits examination. Jacob, on his way home after serving Laban, wrestled with an angel until the break of day. Although Jacob was wounded in the thigh during the struggle, he did not release his hold on the angel until the latter gave him a blessing and changed Jacob's name to Israel. Jacob called the place of struggle Peniel, "face of God," for, he said, "I have seen God face to face."

It is pertinent that Freud was very fond of a play by the contemporary Austrian Richard Beer-Hofmann, which harked back to Jacob's contest (Schur, 1972, 208). In the famous conclusion of "Beyond the Pleasure Principle," Freud cites two verses from a poem alluding to Jacob's struggle, and on several other critical occasions in his life Freud depicted his ongoing struggle with the forces of the unconscious by invoking Jacob's encounter with the angel. There was, first of all, Freud's famous Irma dream, which he had in July 1895. In it, he describes not himself but Breuer as a limping antihero (Freud, 1900, 107, 112). The next month Freud conflated, however briefly, the stories of Jacob wrestling the angel and Moses climbing Mount Nebo in sight of the Promised Land, and he identified with both heroes (Freud, 1985, 135). More to our own purposes, in a letter he sent shortly before taking Dora into treatment, Freud identifies Fliess with Jacob and then spells out his own identification with the Israelite hero: "The beauty of [your book]. . . will give you the first compensation for your arduous wrestling with the demon. . . . When it appeared that my breath would fail me in the wrestling match, I asked the angel to desist; and that is what he has done since then. But I did not turn out to be the stronger, although since then I have been limping noticeably" (Freud, 1985, 412). In the same letter, let us note, Freud hedged in referring to the "possibly feminine" part of himself that required male friendship.

Finally, the Dora case. Just after labeling Dora's termination of the treatment "an unmistakable act of vengeance" (109), Freud declares that no one struggling with the demons in the human breast can survive unscathed. He and Dora limped in different ways. As we shall see, a physical injury perhaps was the cause of her lameness, whereas Freud limped after his struggle with her, when he was figuratively wounded in the thigh—castrated. But here, contrary to his other uses of the Jacob legend, he changed his opponent from angel to demon. She dragged Freud down into the tangling shades of bisexuality and transference.

3

Trauma, Symptoms, and Diagnosis

It is merely a case of "petite hystérie."

The original title of the Dora case, "Dreams and Hysteria: A Fragment of an Analysis," encapsulates some of its major clinical aims. In sum, Freud undertook to show how the analysis of dreams could be used in treatment to explain the etiology of hysteria and its symptomatic aftermath. He had already underscored the impact of trauma and conflict in *Studies on Hysteria*; and in publications shortly following that one, he added that all hysteria had a sexual etiology. In the Dora case, the supplement to *The Interpretation of Dreams*, Freud continued to explore his understanding of psychoneurosis and its inscription on the textual nightlife of our dreams.

Freud never offered a systematic explanation of the oedipal complex; he developed his theory throughout his life, and in *Three Essays on the Theory of Sexuality* he held that infantile sexuality remained basically autoerotic, the oedipal object choice not fully taking place until puberty (Pontalis and Laplanche, 1968). In the Dora case itself Freud does not give us an integrated picture of oedipal and hysterical issues; rather, his ongoing discussion emerges as a free-floating response to the material at hand, much the way symptoms are cleared up piecemeal (12). In analyzing Dora as a very young child or as a teenager, Freud now discusses normal and pathological development, now differentiates hysteria from other neuroses and from perversion.

In a summary statement Freud outlines his idea of psycho-pathogenesis. Pathological oedipal development occurs when sexual constitution marks a child out for a neurosis; the child develops prematurely and has a craving for love; and other influences join to lead to a fixation of rudimentary love that is on a par with sexual inclination. Those influences are genital sensations either appearing spontaneously or resulting from masturbation or seduction (56–57 and n.). In this groping oedipal formulation Freud admits that disruptive genital sensation can arise from widely differing sources.[1]

The offspring of syphilitic parents have a strong constitutional disposition toward neurosis. In Dora's case that factor carried more weight than the mental disposition inherited from both sides of her family. Freud adds that children whose constitution marks them out for neurosis *and* who develop prematurely acquire an early sexual fixation. To restate this in slightly different words: very intense love such as Dora's for her father is characteristic of those who are disposed constitutionally to neurosis and whose sexuality develops prematurely. A childhood history of premature sexual enjoyment determines two responses to love in adulthood: either an abandonment that borders on perversity or a neurotic repudiation. Constitution decides which response will predominate (87–88).

In the etiological specificity of hysteria as a pathological disorder, a prerequisite psychic trauma activates the reversal of af-

---

1. Blass (1992, 168, 177, 180) misreads Freud's postulate as referring exclusively to external actuality as opposed to an internal force. In her thoughtful article Blass insists that Freud gradually abandoned the seduction hypothesis and that likewise in the Dora case he was groping toward an oedipal formulation but without ever reaching it. Blass overstates her position about the Dora case, however, and attributes more theoretical revisions to Freud than I would grant. Blass pushes her argument for Freud's hesitancy too far, as when she collapses his former hesitation (which he delivers in the past perfect tense) with his present resolution (206/46–47). She (165) likewise tries to draw too much from the word "inexperienced" in the English translation, which is inadequate to the subtlety of the German *unerfahrenes*. In German there are two words for "experience," *Erlebnis*, meaning an experience that is simply lived or witnessed, and *Erfahrung*, meaning the lessons or wisdom drawn from that experience. On the positive side, Blass explores with astuteness Freud's novel concept of reactive reinforcement (168–169, 178, 181, 183).

fect, whereby pleasure is turned into unpleasurable feeling. Conflictual memories involved in that trauma are then repressed. The motive forces forming the symptoms of hysteria derive their vitality "not only from repressed *normal* sexuality but also from unconscious perverse activities" (51). The compliance of one of the bodily organs affords an outlet to unconscious psychic processes, and it is precisely the specificity of a somatic factor accompanying a psychic one that differentiates hysterical symptoms from those of other neuroses. In many instances the somatic part of a later hysterical symptom must have an infantile prototype. For example, an organically determined irritation of Dora's throat formed the lowest stratum. That irritation in an erotogenic zone was suitable to express excited states of the libido; it was brought to fixation by its first psychic coating: Dora's imitation of her father (compare also Freud's idea that a woman's genital catarrh or leucorrhea forms an organic base that later receives the psychic coating of her repugnance or disgust). When children or adults are masturbating, they rarely have hysterical symptoms; with adults, if their libido is strong, hysterical symptoms and diminished masturbation can co-occur (79 and n.).

So far so good, but it is precisely in the details of the psychosexual sphere that Freud is theoretically inconsistent. On one hand, he sees an inherent somatic factor as necessary in differentiating hysteria from other neuroses. On the other hand, he withdraws the necessity of a somatic component in hysteria when he finds that in some incidents calling for a preponderantly sexual excitement, any child incurring a lack of pleasure would be hysterical, even if that child could not produce any somatic symptoms. Another, longer example: near the start of his case history Freud merely asserts that hysterical symptoms represent a person's most secret and repressed wishes; specifying the repressed content some pages later, he states that every symptom constitutes the realization of a sexual situation; he then restricts his postulate to the "majority" of hysterical symptoms; and finally he returns to his universal tenet that hysterical symptoms "are nothing else than *the patient's sexual activity*" (115; see also 7–8, 72, 103n).

In the Dora case, conviction, unfounded inferences, and fiction characterize Freud's development of his hypotheses. He shows himself as a man ablaze with a mission, and it is indeed fascinating to see how tirelessly his mind works and how he shifts back and forth from cognition to fantasy. Again and again, we are offered coherence, but without firm evidence that would both confirm it and prove its correspondence with reality. There was no adequacy in kneading her wants.

A main thrust of Freud's therapeutic strategy was to identify and reconstruct Dora's traumatic experiences: in addition to the two later traumas in Dora's life, Freud drew up a childhood primal scene whose impact approached that of a trauma (we may wonder whether there were other traumas initiated by Hans, Philip, or some other).[2] As I have suggested, a chronological blurring and unstable developmental referentiality vitiate Freud's account, so that at times we do not know whether he is talking about a younger or an older Dora. With good reason, we suspect that her varying appellation in the case history—female person, child, girl, woman, lady—reveals Freud's countertransferential confusion over both the developmental attainment of his patient and her accountability.

It is in keeping with his clinical designs that Freud accorded selective consideration to the symptoms that Dora later presented: dyspnea, tussis nervosa, aphonia, migraines, depression, unsociability, and taedium vitae. He does not dwell on the unsociability and depression, and he bypasses the taedium vitae except to say that it was probably simulated. And he gives merely passing attention to the possibly hysterical nature of the migraines that Dora suffered from between the ages of twelve and sixteen. By contrast, Dora's symptoms of dyspnea, tussis nervosa, and aphonia monopolize Freud's analytic attention. He posits that their sequential outbreak, along with a perduring incapacity to

2. It is indeed curious that, on one hand, Freud also made much of the primal scene in his case history of the Wolf Man, who had a room of his own in his parents' palatial mansion; on the other hand, Freud did not examine the place of the real primal scene in the Rat Man's case history, even though he slept in the parental bedroom when a child (1909, 161).

love, resulted from the nefarious interaction between Dora's primal scene and her masturbation experiences.

Dora's Quasi Trauma and Childhood Symptoms

Setting his stakes tremendously high, Freud believed that Dora fell ill from masturbation, to which he attributed a powerful series of immediate and deferred effects in her childhood and adolescence.[3] The circumstantial evidence for Dora's masturbation lies mostly on a few skimpy statements that Freud managed to extract about her early enuresis and leucorrhea. Freud wove these physical symptoms into his narrative about a series of Dora's childhood impressions that "had an effect analogous to that of a trauma" (27). As we shall see, however, Freud's exposition is far from convincing.

Dora recalled that she resumed bedwetting when she was about seven. In Freud's mind, it was most likely caused by masturbation (72, 74). Linking her autoerotic acts with fantasies about her father, Freud relates that Philip "often" woke her up to prevent her from bedwetting (73n and 89). In spite of Freud's assumption, in the Bauer household that paternal custom was not likely. Philip could hardly have been available to offer his daughter bedside attention when he himself, ailing with tuberculosis, demanded attention, and had moved with his whole family shortly before to Merano. Dora's hygiene would more likely have been attended to by her mother, whose habits of obsessive cleanliness were a trial to her household—she had family members remove their shoes before entering, insisted on their absence during the day of her weekly "spring" cleaning, locked up her husband's cigars, and so on.

Freud considered leucorrhea as another sign of infantile mas-

3. See the minutes of the Vienna Psychoanalytic Society for November 11, 1908: "If a female hysteric is made angry, she suffers an attack. It is a substitute for masturbation—for sexual activity in general. She now gets a hysterical attack in the same set of circumstances that previously caused her to masturbate" (Nunberg and Federn, 1967, 51).

turbation. For him, Dora's early discharge constituted an "admission [*Eingeständnis*] that she had masturbated in childhood" (237/75): "She was afflicted with a catarrh (leucorrhea) whose beginning, she said, she could not remember. . . . I met her halfway by assuring her that in my view the occurrence of leucorrhea in young girls pointed primarily to masturbation, and I considered that all the other causes which were commonly assigned to that complaint were put in the background by masturbation. I added that she was now on the way to finding an answer to her own question of why it was precisely that she had fallen ill—by confessing [*Eingeständnis*] that she had masturbated, probably in childhood" (238/76). Two points merit comment. In his overdetermined idiolect, Freud equates possible revelation with assured confession, and inference with conclusive proof: Dora was "confessing" her masturbation. Next, the very important comma before "probably in childhood," found also in the German text, grammatically implies that the so-called confession probably referred to Dora's childhood. Yet this statement, allowing the possibility that Dora did *not* masturbate in childhood, contradicts Freud's certitude about the matter a page earlier and undermines the thrust of his etiological theory in the case.

A few days later, after Dora denied having any memory of masturbation, she put her fingers into her double-bladed purse while she was on the couch, an act regarded by Freud as "a further step towards the confession" (238/76; the German word *Geständnis*, which Freud now uses for "confession," has legal implications). Three pages later, we find Freud sticking to his supposition despite Dora's continued disagreement: "And indeed, Dora no longer denied my supposition, although she still remembered nothing" (79). He spelled out his conviction this way: "The reproaches against her father for having made her ill, together with the self-reproach underlying them, the leucorrhoea, the playing with the reticule, the bedwetting after her sixth year, the secret which she would not allow the doctors to tear from her—the circumstantial evidence of her having masturbated in her childhood seems to me to be complete and without a flaw" (78).

During the next phase of his argument Freud pauses to savor a reconstruction of Dora's masturbation. Her symptomatic acts gave him "good reasons for supposing" (79) that Dora had overheard her parents in coitus, an event that was the precipitating cause of her dyspnea. Right after recording that supposition, Freud takes off in flights of fantasy, portraying both the grand design and minor details of a plot. According to the core of Freud's reconstruction, Dora's first asthmatic attack expressed a wish for her absent father to return, contained the memory that her father was forbidden to overexert himself or to climb mountains, provided evidence of Dora's memory that he had harmed himself during coitus that night, and manifested a worry that in masturbating to orgasm she might have overexerted herself—an event followed by an intensified dyspnea. The gratuitous suppositions in the content and sequence of Freud's reconstructions are evident: that the eight-year-old Dora's previous masturbation had a resultant orgasm, and that the traumalike primal scene was followed by the cessation of her masturbation and the onset of dyspnea— her first hysterical symptom.

After huffing and puffing and telling Dora and us that she became ill because of masturbation, Freud goes on to refuse a yes or no answer about the onanistic etiology of Dora's hysteria. Instead, he now restricts himself to the postulate that the practice is not accidental or immaterial to Dora's clinical picture (81–82). But his reserve does not hold for long. With noted certitude Freud maintains that Dora's premature masturbatory enjoyment and its immediate consequences (enuresis, catarrh, and disgust) led her to reproach her father, repress her love for Hans, and suffer from neurosis (87–88). In Freud's lights, unbeknown to Dora while she was masturbating, the hand of Fate was busy writing another fortune for her. But unbeknown to Freud, he himself was already sketching the bleakest notes for his "Civilization and Its Discontents," published three decades later.

Dora's coughing and aphonia make a complicated story. And, the countless readings of the case history notwithstanding, a contradiction in Freud's temporal account of Dora's symptoms has remained undetected. We learn first that Dora's simultaneous coughing and aphonia started when she was about twelve, an occurrence accepted by Strachey in his chronological table (compare 6 and 22). But several pages later in the case history Freud seems to have forgotten this dating and now, in a capital discrepancy, has Dora's cough and aphonia start in her eighth year (27).

Freud's account is also questionable in connection with the accuracy of Dora's memory about limited units of time in the far past. We are told that Peppina felt well during her husband's absence and ill upon his return and that Dora talked of experiencing her own alternations between good and bad health "during the first years" in Merano (39). After floating the question about whether Hans's absence might have determined the alternations in Dora's health, Freud answers himself with a reckless inference: "If this were so, it must be possible to discover some coincidence or other which would betray the fact. I asked her what the average length of these attacks had been. 'From three to six weeks, perhaps.' How long had Herr K.'s absences lasted? 'Three to six weeks, too,' she was obliged to admit. *Her illness was therefore a demonstration of her love for K.*" (39, my italics). Freud then adds that the correspondence between Dora's attacks and Hans's absences initially held good, but that later she unconsciously disrupted the correspondence to keep her love secret.[4]

Given that Dora stayed in Merano from age six to seventeen, her "first years" there would accord with Freud's earlier dating for her cough—that is, when she was eight. His narrative of her love

4. Freud confuses this whole subject in his narrative: Dora's tussis nervosa began at age eight (27) or twelve (12), and each attack lasted for three to five weeks (22) or three to six weeks (39). The correlative onset of aphonia with coughing also lacks clarity: aphonia occurred during the first half of each coughing attack "in the last years" (Strachey inserts "few" between "last" and "years," 180/22). In Dora's early years in Merano her aphonia, occurring during the first half of each coughing attack, coincided with Hans's absence. Upon his return her coughing continued but her aphonia ceased. Later it became necessary for Dora to obscure the coincidence of her attacks with Hans's absences (39–40). To the extent that the ground of Dora's psychic life was her love 'for not Hans but Peppina, her aphonia, concurring with his absence, had more to do with being alone with Peppina (cf. Lacan, 1956, 3:197).

for Hans and her calculated simulation of sickness fits better with the age of twelve as the onset of coughing. The discrepancy in these dates alerts us to other temporal oddities in his account. Freud attributed an adultomorphic maturity to her symptomatology and to her defensive secrecy about her "love"; he amplified the infatuation of an eight-year-old or twelve-year-old child into an adult response. Then again, could the seventeen- or eighteen-year-old Dora have remembered so far back in her childhood about the specific duration of her attacks and Hans's absences? Dora's life story and Freud's confused report do not always mesh.

The Shop Trauma

When the middle-aged pedophilic Hans suddenly clasped the thirteen-year-old Dora, she must have been unsuspecting and all the more traumatized. If she conformed to the statistical norm, she would not have begun menstruating for another three years, the average age of menarche for the European female at the time being about sixteen and three-quarter years. This circumstance, along with the generally earlier age at marriage, aggravated the plight of young women, who were treated until marriage like children by their parents and then likewise after marriage by their husbands.[5] Dora would have been much afflicted by her first trauma, then. Three versions have come down to us.

First is Freud's report of Dora's version, which requires full citation.

> Dora told me of an earlier episode with Herr K., which was even better calculated to act as a sexual trauma. She was fourteen [thirteen] years old at the time. Herr K. had made an arrangement with her and his wife that they should meet him one afternoon at his place of business in the principal square of B—— [Merano] so as to have a view of a church festival. He persuaded his wife,

5. For this reflection and the information about the comparative onset of menarche, see Glenn, 1980, 25–26. The only solid evidence we have about Dora's menses is that she menstruated while mourning her aunt's death in 1899 (*S.E.*, 101).

however, to stay at home, and sent away his clerks, so that he was alone when the girl arrived. When the time for the procession approached, he asked the girl to wait for him at the door which opened on to the staircase leading to the upper story, while he pulled down the outside shutters. He then came back, and, instead of going out by the open door, suddenly clasped the girl to him and pressed a kiss upon her lips. . . . Dora had at that moment a violent feeling of disgust, tore herself free from the man, and hurried past him to the staircase and from there to the street door. She nevertheless continued to meet Herr K. Neither of them ever mentioned the little scene; and according to her account Dora kept it a secret till her confession [*Beichte*, a German word used mostly in an ecclesiastical sense, sometimes in a humorous one]. (27–28)

Three comments are in order. First, in an editorial comment that displays his lack of empathy, Freud trivializes Dora's trauma by identifying it as "little." Second, on July 3, 1896, the Zellenka family moved from the church square to the house right next door to Hans's place of business. Hans would have had to rationalize not inviting his two children, aged five and a half and six and a half, to watch the procession. Freud censored Hans's rationalization, which would have put him in an even worse light. Third, was disgust Dora's principal affect, a kind of secondary revision that was highlighted by Freud, or even his own association? In line with his comment in the Katharina case, it seems plausible that Dora would have reacted to seduction by her father's friend with horror (*Grauen*), repulsion (*Abscheu*), and indignation.[6] But Freud does not allow Dora these emotions in his master plot for the shop trauma. Although easily substituted for the word *disgust*, the much stronger terms *horror, repulsion*, and *panic* do not figure into Freud's linkage between thumbsucking and a putative displacement of disgust onto the mucous membrane. It is ironic that when

6. In commenting on his treatment of the eighteen-year-old Katharina, whose father sexually approached her when she was fourteen, Freud (1893–1895, 127) says: "I had found often enough that in girls anxiety was a consequence of the horror by which a virginal mind is overcome when it is faced for the first time with the world of sexuality."

he anticipates the reactions of medical readers to his open sexual dialogue with Dora, he pictures such varied affects as horror, indignation, and sexual excitement, but not disgust (48–49). The second version of the shop trauma, Freud's own version, has five subplots.

1. Freud's phallocentric reconstruction serves a concoction of projective wish-fulfillment featuring the erectile penis: "I believe that during the man's passionate embrace she felt not merely his kiss upon her lips but also the pressure of his erect member against her body" (30). Freud's parodic simplification does not honor the overdetermination of psychic acts. As early as 1896, in "The Aetiology of Hysteria" (1896a), Freud explained that hysteria, rather than arising from a single experience, is overdetermined; and he compared that overdetermination to a genealogical tree in which there has been plentiful intermarriage.

Freud repeats his tenet of overdeterminism on many pages in the Dora case history, except when he offers his unifactorial, anti-polysemous reconstruction that puts Dora in a male-dominated fantasy. Freud's portrayal of Dora's overdetermined symptomatic reaction of disgust curiously contrasts with his fantasy about her underdetermined sexual excitement. Might that interpretation of undetermination have arisen from Freud's ambivalence toward his patient "of intelligence and engaging looks" (23), an ambivalence which he then represses in part and cloaks in a simplified projection? In other words, might his monocausal explanation have been a projection of his own wishes about her excitability?[7]

7. Compare Gay (1988, 249): "Freud was not insinuating that Dora should have yielded to Herr K.'s importunities at fourteen—or, for that matter, at sixteen. But he thought it only obvious that such an encounter should generate a measure of sexual arousal, and that Dora's response was a symptom of her hysteria." But Freud did fantasize that Dora already had a measure of sexual arousal and reacted neurotically in stopping it. He also insisted that she was tempted to yield to Hans (70, 73, 85, 86, 88), and he held that, in contradistinction with the yielding governess with whom Dora identified, Dora was neurotically repudiating her sexuality. Note, too, Freud's suggestion upon hearing that Hans had given Dora a present of jewelry: "Then a return-present would have been very appropriate. Perhaps you do not know that 'jewel-case' is a favorite expression for the same thing that you alluded to not long ago by means of the reticule you were wearing —for the female genitals, I mean" (69).

Sliding from privileged competence to silently synonymizing competence with omniscience, Freud paints a scene between two sexually wound-up robots, one perfectly oiled; and the other, Dora, should have reacted in no other way but with excitement. Much to his patriarchal displeasure, Dora resisted Hans's sexual advance, and, contrary to Freud's gratuitous assumption, in the possibly two or three seconds of manhandling Dora, Hans might not have been erectile at all.

2. Stretching out his patriarchal fantasy, Freud maintains the probability that Dora became so excited that her vagina swelled: "The pressure of the erect member probably led to an analogous change in the corresponding female organ, the clitoris" (30). Disregarding Dora's traumatic state, Freud imagined her like a match, which, once struck, should have kindled immediately. Freud's expectation of Dora's excitability is all the more unreasonable in that he traced the origins of Dora's neurotic repudiation of sexuality not to the shop trauma but to her childhood masturbation many years earlier. Furthermore, that Dora was homosexual at her deepest psychic level certainly intensified her repudiation of heterosexual impulses. We may wonder whether Dora was ever able to be sexually excited by men. We may recall, too, Deutsch's report that Dora remained frigid and distrustful of men when she was a married adult.

3. Only once during his reconstruction does Freud descend from certainty to possibility—namely, when he suspects that Dora may have imagined that all men, including Hans, resembled her father in various psychological and physical ways: "The same governess whom Dora cast off on account of her faithlessness had, from her own experience of life, propounded to Dora the view that all men were frivolous and untrustworthy. To Dora that must mean that all men were like her father. . . . She might therefore have imagined to herself that all men suffered from venereal disease" (84). Whereas Freud permits himself to reveal doubts about relatively incidental matters, his hyperinvested argumentation stands out when he holds on to the highest certitude for essential matters and replaces plausibility with narrative inev-

itability. His definitive attitude toward the trauma has none of the tentativeness of his reconstruction of the Wolf Man's trauma years later.

4. Freud finally advances his own questionable conception of how a healthy fourteen-year-old girl (a year older than Dora actually was) would react in similar circumstances: the kissing episode "was surely just the situation to call up a distinct feeling of sexual excitement in a girl of fourteen who had never before been approached [*unberührten*]" (186/28).[8] Flushing out the cynicism in his fantasy about pedophilia and youthful virginity, Freud adds that in a situation similar to Dora's, any young female would be "completely" hysterical if her aroused feelings were not "preponderantly" sexual. We cannot make light of Freud's cynical belief that the kiss would have been repeated if the "girl" had yielded.[9]

5. In following Dora's later reactions, Freud draws up a scene of men having an affectionate conversation in public, and he describes her as fantasizing that these men are sexually excited: "For some time afterwards, however, she avoided being alone with Herr K. . . . [There subsequently arose] her unwillingness to walk past any man whom she saw engaged in eager or affectionate conversation with a lady. . . . The compulsive piece of behavior which I have mentioned was formed as though it were derived from the undistorted recollection of the scene: she did not like walking past any man who she thought was in a state of sexual excitement, because she wanted to avoid seeing for a second time the somatic sign which accompanies it. . . . Her avoidance [*Scheu*] of men who might possibly be in a state of sexual excitement follows the mechanism of a phobia" (186–189/28–31).[10] In short, Dora was hemmed in by her father's preposterous self-

---

8. The German word *unberührten* means "untouched" and is used in the figurative sense of "virginal" (the rendering in *S.E.* in the sense of unapproached is a mistranslation: despite being approached by Hans, Dora remained virginal).

9. In *S.E.*, "girl"· (*Mädchen*, 236/74) is translated simply as "she."

10. Strachey mistranslates *Scheu*, which is better rendered as "nervousness": Dora manifested a nervousness of men in a possible state of excitement.

serving denial of the lake scene on one side and, on the other, by Freud's own fantastical reconstruction of profuse tumescence.

Finally, other analytic versions of the shop trauma exist, although from 1905 to 1962 there appears to have been little substantial criticism of Freud's case history.[11] If, for example, Jung had written an interpretation of the lake scene in 1905 that had then been criticized by Freud for its lack of basic decency, it is hardly speculation to state that psychoanalytic journals, comforted by Freud's endorsement, would have contained scathing criticisms of Jung's brutishness from early on.

Karl Abraham's laudatory review (1909), the earliest by a psychoanalyst, contained no reservations: "This case history is a lucid demonstration of the role of dream interpretation in psychoanalysis and vindicates its practical significance. It also brings to light the formidable resistance of hysterics to the explication of their unconscious impulses."[12] Jones (1955) was typically sycophantic: "There is no analyst who would not be proud to have unraveled so much of a difficult case in that short time. . . . Dora was a disagreeable creature who consistently put revenge before love; it was the same motive that led her to break off the treatment prematurely." He trilled even louder: "This first case history of Freud's has for years served as a model for students of psychoanalysis, and although our knowledge has greatly progressed since then, it makes today as interesting reading as ever. . . . Here

11. There are two exceptions. The first criticism is in Lacan's essay (1952); he faulted Freud on issues of transference and sexual identity but, remarkably, not for mistreating Dora. The second criticism is by Wolstein (1954), who advanced the idea that Dora's most serious problem was rooted in the loveless relationship with her mother and that Freud missed many elements in Dora's transference. Wolstein, however, did not specifically object to Freud's handling of the trauma as such. In one additional place Wolstein (55) tentatively offered a reflection that would be the heart of Erikson's (1964) criticism: Dora "may actually have wanted to maintain some remnants of integrity in an inter-familial situation which certainly did not overflow with it."

12. This essay is found in Kiell, 1988, 295–296. Pertinently, there are two early nonanalysts, writing reviews in 1905 and 1906, who criticize Freud's analysis of Dora's sexual response during the shop trauma (Kiell, 1988, 286–294).

was a man who not only listened closely to every word his patient spoke but regarded each such utterance as every whit as definite and as in need of correlation as the phenomena of the physical world" (255–257). Erikson (1964) was the first to criticize Freud's treatment globally and to have the courage and common sense to say that Hans "propositioned her [Dora] quite unequivocally." Erikson correctly said of Deutsch's portrait of Dora that it was "as unfavorable as may be seen in clinical annals."[13]

In her shop trauma Dora was sexually attacked. The attack was iatrogenically repeated by Freud and then by the submissive psychoanalytic community. The early blind acceptance of the Dora case might even have contributed its share to Freud's primal horde theory. In therapy and in his writing he would continue to abuse Dora and effect acceptance of his version by his colleagues and later analysts. The interpretive tradition of psychoanalysis kept up the primal horde dynamic, whereby brothers submitted to what the father wanted to do with women. If the Dora case was truly a clinically organizing experience in Freud's relations with women, it was also an untoward organizing experience in the psychoanalytic movement. That it has since become an organizing experience for feminist critics is all to the good.

The Lakeside Trauma

By paying careful attention to Freud's rhetorical presentation of Dora's second trauma we can understand how he handled her. In this regard, let us not forget a point that Freud glosses over: the mental condition of the fifteen-year-old Dora just prior to her trauma. On the way to the lake, the hoarse, coughing adolescent consulted Freud, who found her to be "unmistakably neurotic." Without further commentary, Freud also declares that in spite of

13. Because the Dora case was originally published in 1905, we easily calculate from Erikson's 1958 statements (*Daedalus*, 87:65–87) that it took fifty-three years of psychoanalytic history before "Freud's lack of decency" was singled out in print. Erikson's essay is more widely known through its expanded version in *Insight and Responsibility* (1964), from which I cite.

Dora's cough having lasted unusually long, at the time of consultation it disappeared "spontaneously." We may ask ourselves, however, what relation there was between Dora's spontaneous remission and the trauma that took place shortly after the consultation (22, 25).

Freud had a distorted idea of gallantry and its merited reward. Consider this scenario: A middle-aged married man addressing a young teenager and former victim of his sexual molestation remarks as an the overture that he gets nothing sexual from his wife. The teenager smacks the would-be adulterer and statutory rapist in the face. According to Freud, she is the brutal one. She should have appreciated the love offer, for it was "not in the least" tactless or offensive (*keineswegs*, 197n/38n).[14]

If Dora's reported account of the first trauma contained most of the episodic facts, her reported account of the second trauma is initially sparse, confined to one sentence in Freud's narrative: "Herr K. had had the audacity to make her a proposal [*Liebesantrag*; read: "overture of love"] while they were on a walk after a trip upon the lake" (184/25). It seems, however, that "overture of love" in this sentence belongs to Freud alone and that he has already editorialized in the account. Slightly later in the narrative, we hear what sounds like Dora, but in the voice of her doubting father: "I myself believe that Dora's tale of the man's immoral suggestions is a phantasy that has forced its way into her mind" (184/26). (Strachey's "immoral suggestions" waters down *Zumu-*

14. The superlative force of Freud's charge in lessened in *S.E.* by the translation of *keineswegs* by the simple negative "neither. . . nor"). Freud's charge comes across all the more chillingly in the German text, which stresses Dora's youth, for both she and Freud refer to her parents as "Mom" and "Dad."

Freud offers an overdetermined explanation for Dora's refusal, much as he did for her repudiation of sexuality in the first trauma: "There was a conflict within her between a temptation to yield to the man's proposal and a composite force rebelling against that feeling. This latter force was made up of motives of respectability and good sense, of hostile feelings caused by the governess's disclosures (jealousy and wounded pride) . . . and of a neurotic element, namely, the tendency to a repudiation of sexuality which was already présent in her and was based on her childhood history. Her love for her father, which she summoned up to protect her against the temptation, had its origin in this same childhood history" (88–89).

tung, which means "impertinence" [the same mistranslation appears on 269/106]. The rest of the disembodied translation in the *Standard Edition*—Dora's fantasy "forced its way into her mind"—eliminates the impact of the German "sich ihr aufgedrängt hat" [forced itself upon her].) In the original German, Philip mocks Dora's account of Hans's imposition by saying that a fantasy of her own forced itself upon her; that is, Dora's fantasy about Hans's infringement upon her reenacts upon herself that very encroachment.

An interpretive crux of the case history deserves to be highlighted at this juncture: what Freud calls an overture of love and Dora calls an impertinent demand or proposition is called suggestions in the *Standard Edition.* Freud is already hanging Dora, depicting her as forced not by Hans but by her own fantasies. Freud occasionally comes back to the scene, adding interpretation instead of fact and giving the ambiguous and therefore potentially ameliorative name "overture of love" to the proposition, thereby embellishing Hans's pitch for a young mistress. Freud's bit-by-bit revelation heightens the intrigue of his narrative, which itself becomes a seduction of the reader and counterpoints and yet completes Hans's unsuccessful seduction.

For the next dozen pages, Freud contents himself with filling in the previous and subsequent happenings around the core data, letting us fantasize about the details of the scene itself and about Dora's exaggerated reaction. He then asks in a footnote (though this time explicitly postponing further details), "How could a girl who was in love feel insulted—*as we shall later hear*—by a proposal?" (*Werbung*—more accurately, "courting," 197n/38n, my italics).[15]

Like the small, scattered signs of affection that Freud relates, his narrative of the plot appears in scattered pieces in his text, seductively keeping readers in periodic touch with the seduction scene itself. On one page we read: "No sooner had she grasped

15. I added the highlighted phrase. The translation of the German, *wie wir später hören werden,* is omitted from S.E..

Herr K.'s intention than, without letting him finish what he had to say, she had given him a slap in the face and hurried away. Her behavior must have seemed as incomprehensible to the man after she had left him as to us, for he must long before have gathered from innumerable small signs that he was secure of the girl's affections" (46). And a dozen pages later we read: "She was filled with regret at having rejected the man's proposal [*Antrag*; read: "overture"], and with longing for his company and all the little signs of his affection; while on the other hand these feelings of tenderness and longing were combated by powerful forces, among which her pride was one of the most obvious" (58). In his criticism of Dora, Freud continues to barb his arrows. He invites us join him in emphathizing with Hans, for Dora's refusal of Hans should be incomprehensible to all.

Only at the time of Dora's second dream, reported three days before the end of the treatment, was Freud "beginning to realize" that Hans himself did not regard his "courting as a mere frivolous attempt at seduction."[16] Thus, *throughout most of the treatment, Freud thought that at the lake scene the "unmistakably neurotic" Dora was being hoodwinked by the insincere Hans. Only at the very end of the treatment did Freud think that the love overture was a proposal and not a proposition.* Until this late stage, therefore, Freud's blanket condemnation of the fifteen-year-old girl's refusal was strictly on the grounds of her alleged sexual inhibition. Since for Freud the putative suavity of a pedophilic father was more honorable than his insincerity, Dora should have yielded (and pretended, much like the colluding adults around her?).

But even retrospectively, how could Freud say that Hans's overture was "in earnest" (107) and that he was not merely on the make? Just shortly before, he had baited his governess and dumped her. When the subject of divorce came up between him and his wife, as it often did, he would refuse on account of his affection for his children (37). Only a year or so later, when the

---

16. I have followed Strachey's text except for his translation of *Werbung* (257/95) as "proposal" instead of "courting."

Bauers moved to Reichenburg, did Hans want to divorce and his wife did not (107).

Let us return to Hans's follow-up to his traumatization of Dora. She recounted the next incident: "In the afternoon after our trip on the lake, from which we (Herr K. and I) returned at midday, I had gone to lie down as usual on the sofa in the bedroom to have a short sleep. I suddenly awoke and saw Herr. K. standing beside me. . . . He said he was not going to be prevented from coming into his own bedroom when he wanted; besides, there was something he wanted to fetch. . . . The next morning I locked myself in while I was dressing. That afternoon, when I wanted to lock myself in so as to lie down again on the sofa, the key was gone. I was convinced that Herr K. had removed it" (66). Whether Freud thought that Hans's behavior was again "neither tactless nor offensive," we do not know. He also passed another fact over in silence: that Dora, once fond of jewelry, never wore any after the summer trauma (68)—perhaps, we may muse, because of her decision not to wear anything reminiscent of Hans's gifts and because of her phobic reaction to appearing attractive. Led on by his gender-biased designations, Freud labeled Hans's aggressive and boorish attitudes as tactful and Dora's active resistance unhealthy and spiteful.

At the lake Dora learned that while Hans was "ardently courting" (*sehr umwerben*, 268/105) his children's governess, he said, "I get nothing out of my wife." Then he recycled his one-line approach with Dora shortly afterward. Nonetheless, Freud labeled his overture as far from frivolous: "Herr K.'s exordium had been somewhat serious; but she had not let him finish what he had to say. No sooner had she grasped the purport of his words than she had slapped him" (98). Freud himself symbolically slaps the fifteen-year-old girl for reporting the incident to her mother: "A normal girl, I am inclined to think, will finish off a situation of this kind by herself" (95).[17]

17. "Finish off" is my translation of *wird . . . fertig* (257/95); compare Strachey's weaker expression, "will deal with."

At this point we must ask, Was Hans acting with any decency to the young governess a few days before he repeated the line to Dora? He had recently slept with the governess of his children, occasioned her family's rejection of her, and then spurned her. After he tried to hustle Dora, was he acting decently to go a little later into her unlocked room and insist that he could go wherever he wanted? And whoever did so, was it decent to steal the key that could have guaranteed Dora's privacy? Neither Philip nor Peppina appears in Freud's account of the day of the trauma and the next day, when the key was missing. Chances are that if Philip had been around in the afternoon, Hans would not have barged into the room where Dora was sleeping and claimed the room as his. Philip was staying elsewhere, in a hotel, and Peppina set out early in the mornings "so as to go on expeditions with him" (67). How complicitous they were with Hans's machinations that day is an open question. At any event, was it decent several weeks later, in answering Philip's accusation, for Hans to attack Dora as prurient and fanciful? Hans pursued his intentions with renewed energy by giving Dora a Christmas present the same year. Was Hans decent even once?

The grotesqueness of Freud's attitude to Dora's trauma emerges best in a belated irony. When Freud's eighteen-year-old daughter Anna was planning to visit England, where she was to be hosted by the sexually entrepreneurial Jones, Freud apparently did not think she was "normal" enough to deal with the situation by herself. The protective father wrote a letter telling Jones to keep his distance: "She is the most gifted and accomplished of my children and a valuable character besides. Full of interest for learning, seeing sights, and getting to understand the world. She does not claim to be treated as a woman, being still far away from sexual longings and rather refusing man. There is an outspoken understanding between me and her that she should not consider marriage or the preliminaries before she gets 2 or 3 years older. I don't think she will break the treaty" (Freud, 1993a, 294). In sum, if Freud turned a deaf ear to the overdetermined possibility that Hans was taking revenge on Dora's encroaching father by pursuing Dora, he was alert to the possibility of losing his daughter "in a clear act of revenge" (*an einen deutlichen Racheakt*) on Jones's part (Freud, letter of July 17, 1914, to Ferenczi; Sigmund Freud Collection, Library of Congress).

Having treated various clinical elements ranging from Dora's transference and bisexuality to her symptoms and trauma, we are equipped to deal with diagnostic issues.[18] Dora had a fragile hysterical personality organization—one could even say a borderline personality disorder with a range of features, including structural weakness of the ego and a certain lability of affect.[19] Significant as well as dramatic conversion phenomena, which increased with her maturity, offer evidence of deficient psychic elaboration. She responded to them with the classic *belle indifférence*: she complained about other people, not about her symptoms.[20]

Dora was beset by a torrent of unstable and contradictory identifications characterized by displacements and condensations of preoedipal and oedipal elements. Within the maelstrom she circulated phantasmally in a series of erotic triangles: those of her parents, the Zellenkas, her father and Peppina, her father and his governess, Hans and his governess. In refusing to wear jewelry after the lakeside trauma and in rejecting Hans, Dora herself

18. By placing self-reproach at the center of Dora's hysterical character, Freud distanced himself from his Draft K, dated 1896, in which he claimed that conflict was the pathological aberration of hysteria, and self-reproach the pathological aberration of obsessional neurosis (Freud, 1985, 162).

19. For the borderline diagnosis of Dora, see Meissner (1984–1985) and Slipp (1977). Slipp opines that had Dora not been exploited and abandoned by her father, she would have remained neurotically hysterical; instead, thrown back to an identification with her masochistic, helpless mother, she became borderline with depressive and paranoid features.

20. Compare Fain, 1968, 682–683, 709–711; David and de M'Uzan, 1968, 697–707; and David, 1974. The psychosomaticians David and de M'Uzan raise interesting questions: Can somatic compliance have its own evolution that more or less resists psychic integration? If—as Freud says in one passage—Dora's cough and migraine started to evolve simultaneously (22), might two fantasies have been at work, or did one fantasy express itself fully in the cough and inhibitedly in the migraine? Might object relations have acted as a determinant upon Dora's migraine in that it broke out at the same time as the onset of Philip's confusional state?

perceived the link between the exchange of gifts and the exchange of women. Freud trained his primary clinical focus on a derivative of the positive oedipal complex, that is, Dora's attraction to Hans. In contrast, clinical stress on the negative oedipal complex would hold Dora's unconscious identification and hostility with her father, as well as a wish to copulate with his beloved Peppina, who herself was a maternal displacement.[21]

A masochistic bond of victimization developed between Dora and her mother; their vaginal catarrh, Dora believed, was an infection transmitted by her father. As it turned out, however, Peppina—Dora's gynecophilic object—became the target of some of unusable maternal identifications. In addition, Dora's jealousy toward her mother, which lasted beyond the infantile period and into her adolescence (90–91), spilled over, affecting her feelings about her father's mistress, the woman with the "adorable white body."[22]

We can easily detect in Dora the dynamic themes of the paranoid process—betrayal, jealousy, projected guilt, and revenge. Although she was often and obviously wronged by her elders, not once did she ever talk about guilt or wrongdoing on her part, a defensive position reinforcing her attitude toward

21. For Lacan, Dora's fundamental problem was that of accepting herself as an object of male desire; in essence, this was a narcissistic dynamic that underlay her admiration of Peppina. Dora, however, always preferred talking about her father, whether dealing with the recent or the remote past, because it was her father who was having sexual relations with Peppina. Moscowitz (1968) and Lewin (1973) have stressed Dora's masculine identification and her sexual longing for her mother. Blos (1979) stresses that Freud was not aware that a cardinal feature of adolescent developmental psychology, the negative oedipal relationship, reaches its conflictual zenith·and resolution only in adolescence. For Krohn and Krohn (1982), Dora's hysterical conflicts stemmed from a regression to the phallic-oedipal phase, in which she cloaked her hatred of her father and actively sought out her mother as the primary libidinal object; the authors see Dora's primary relationship with her mother not as one of undefined longing but as one of specific desires embedded in phallic-oedipal ties.

22. We do not know enough about the psychodynamics of Peppina or Dora's aunt to endorse Decker's (1991, 195) wholesale conclusion: "When manifesting hysterical symptoms, Dora was identifying primarily with her father (and this eventually became her predominant mode of being)."

others as persecutors. In this connection, Dora used revenge to redirect the paranoid and masochistic components of her personality to contend with her jealousy. Otto's comment is sadly believable, though found in Deutsch's untrustworthy report (1957): "It was difficult to get along with her because she distrusted people and attempted to turn them against each other."[23] Adult life did not spare Dora much. Although her heterosexual resiliency was sufficient for her to marry and have a child, her husband and her son deserted her, or so she perceived it. But if they deserted her, her psychosomatic symptoms did not.

In Freud's eyes, bad parenting did not have anything like the causative weight of trauma for her hysteria. Today we understand that Dora's life in her distressful home was cause enough for cumulative trauma and that the cumulative trauma in turn made her more vulnerable to acute trauma. Was Dora's early image of sucking her thumb and tugging at her brother's ear a screen memory that was overdetermined by her desperate self-soothing during her profound isolation and by her abortive wish for an empathic hearing from her parents? We can venture that early disappointment with maternal parenting intensified Dora's alliance—perhaps vengeful in part—with her father and brother. Käthe's fanatical arranging of the house harmed the home. Not only did Dora herself criticize her mother mercilessly, but she encouraged criticism from any quarter, even from her own governess.

The Bauer family became stressed, if not overwhelmed,

23. Meissner's article (1984–1985) offers the best examination of this subject. On another score, Decker has recently been joined by Blum (1994) in asserting that Dora's psychopathology was overdetermined by Jewish conflicts and that her conversion had roots in her Jewish self-hatred and anti-Semitism. Decker's and Blum's unjustified inferences oversimplify the psychology of conversion, be it from Judaism to Christianity or the reverse. In a brilliant review of Decker's book, Kafka (1994, 896) makes these objections: "How representative of Ida Bauer's context are the contemporaneous opinions Decker adduces? Are all assimilations, conversions, and prejudices among Jews to be accounted for in the same way? Do ambition, adaptation, the idiosyncratic personal experiences of childhood before adolescence, the particular capacities for synthesis and originality, among others, enter into Jewish 'self-hatred,' and if so, how?"

when Philip's tuberculosis forced his household to move from Vienna to the health resort of Merano. Six years later, Dora's life was further rocked: her father had his most serious affliction, including confusion and paralysis, and his extramarital liaison became apparent. His and Käthe's lack of sexual satisfaction in marriage could only have intensified Dora's unresolved incestuous conflicts. To boot, and in a reversal of caring roles, for years she behaved like a motherly nurse to her father. Through that role, Dora's oedipal strivings and bodily contact became highly charged. Dora's other adult models of identification—mother, Viennese aunt, and Peppina—also had long histories of illness. The ailing family and friends, together with the sick people thronging the health resort, left their impact on Dora's symptomatology.[24]

For a while she idealized other adult figures in her immediate milieu and reacted to them with mostly positive aspects of her ambivalence to both her parents. She could split the maternal imago into totally bad (Käthe) and totally good (the governess and Peppina). Dora's quest for idealizable adult objects was motivated by preoedipal and oedipal strivings and by attempts at self-restoration to compensate for what she did not receive from her parents. Faced with Käthe's disinterest in her children and Peppina's lessened attention to her own, and evicted from her position as nurse and confidante, Dora was thrown back into her fragile internal world as she strove to construct her own ideal of motherhood.

For a feminine model in her identity formation, she turned from her mother and chose the one favored by her father; thus identifying with Peppina, Dora possessed her father and, to a much lesser extent, Hans. But by having Peppina, her ideal pre-oedipal mother, as an object choice, she also joined with her

24. Seidenberg and Papathomopoulos, 1962. The phasic domination in Dora's desperate idealizations, however, avoids easy discernment. Compare Ornstein (1993, 73n): "Freud's case history as given does not permit a clear-cut recognition of whether Dora's idealizations were archaic, oedipal, or adolescent in nature."

father in blissful accepting her. Dora's identification with Peppina's nurse had contradictory narcissistic aspects; it satisfied her masochistic wish to be allied with demeaned social inferiors. It was essential to Dora, as is evident in her associations to her second dream, to have the Virgin Mother as a model. While retaining her virginity Dora could get no closer to her than by becoming a motherly nurse to substitute children: the Zellenka children, Otto and Clara. Otto afforded Dora the occasion to mother a brother surrogate with the same name; and Clara, the occasion to reverse roles and mother one of the many sick females around her.

In the familial school of abuse, submission was the lot of children, selfishness and betrayal the weaponry of adults. With stratagems and antics of denial the older Bauers and Zellenkas unhoused Dora, impeded her adolescent negotiation of developmentally revived oedipal strivings, thwarted her phase-appropriate quest for an extradomestic embodiment of ideals; increased her conflictual expression of aim-inhibited drives; prevented her from harnessing a healthy idealism with a healthy narcissism; and kept her locked in a hall of distorted mirrors.[25] No longer a baby, she was in the zone of girl-adolescent-woman, that is, permanent servant. Her father could not serve as a model for reality testing, truthfulness, parental reliability and care. Such crucial deficiencies, aggravated by sicknesses over a number of years, character-

25. "The three adults to whom she was closest, whom she loved the most in the world, were apparently conspiring to deny—separately, in tandem, or in concert—the reality of her experience. They were conspiring to deny Dora her reality over reality itself. This betrayal touched upon matters that might easily unhinge the mind of a young person; for the three adults were not only betraying Dora's love and trust alone, they were betraying the structure of the actual world" (Marcus, 1976, 396). See also Rieff (1971, 10): "The sick daughter has a sick father, who has a sick mistress, who has a sick husband, who proposes to the sick daughter as her lover. Dora does not want to hold hands in this charmless circle—although Freud does, at one point, indicate that she should. . . . His entire interpretation of the case—and also his efforts to reindoctrinate Dora in more tolerable attitudes toward her own sexual life—depends upon his limiting the case to Dora when, in fact, from the evidence he himself presents, it is the milieu in which she is constrained to live that is ill."

ize a father incapable of providing parental protection and spon-
soring his daughter's integrated femininity during her oedipal
development. The only men left for Dora to trust were baby boys
and her sibling, Otto.[26] Freud's confused account of Dora's symptoms gives the impression that her complicity lasted longer than it did. His totalizing
adjectives resonate: "During *all* the previous years she had given
every possible assistance to her father's relations with Frau K." (36,
my italics). Actually, her overdetermined complicity began with a
prominent manifestation of her coughing and aphonia and with
her father and Peppina's liaison, when she was twelve, and
stopped with her second trauma, when she was fifteen and able to
see how she had been used all along. Previously, she had mistakenly believed in basic unshakable loyalties. The second trauma
opened her eyes.

Although Dora complemented her paternal object with a
surrogate who was "prepossessing" (29n), younger, and in much
better physical health than her father, she could not enjoy the
adolescent liberty to give indirect vent to her displaced incestuous
wish without falling prey to adult designs. If she learned that Hans
got nothing out of his wife, she also learned that he believed he
would get nothing out of honesty. To her shock she found out that
his easily idealizable positive physical attributes hid a lack of
scruples. Somewhat midway in age between her father and her
brother, Hans represented a combined idealized father and brother
imago; but rather than acting as an idealized non-incestuous
oedipal proxy for her philandering father, Hans had his own
agenda and moved to eroticize his relationship with the daughter
of a wealthy manufacturer. Whereas in his seductive approach he
considered Dora like his governess, he treated her as even less
when she refused him. He calumniated her and disdained her as
having interest in nothing except sexuality.

26. Such a father as Dora had "can be perceived by an adolescent girl as a
danger, as she becomes aware of her own sexual wishes, especially those still close
to oedipal origins. Such feelings are often far more frightening to the adolescent
than to the oedipal child because they can be acted upon in reality" (Scharfman,
1980, 51).

Dora's affectionate feelings curdled into distrust. Her lack of an integrated female identity and body image formed part of her wounded self-esteem; fueled by revived preoedipal rage and blasted by turbulent oedipal relationships, compensatory vengeance blazed forth. We may wonder whether the mounting stress entailed a considerable regression to the oral phase; her coughing, aphonia, and poor eating would lend some credence to that hypothesis. But the primary and secondary gains of her multiple symptomatology offered jumbled solace: mitigated satisfaction of forbidden desires; an active and preemptive self-punishment for them; and a manipulative and castrating control over her neglectful parents. In a self-affirmative sense, among the age-specific developmental tasks she chose to seek the adolescent goals of experiential validation and fidelity—thereby going against the grain of both her familial and societal contexts. Dora challenged her father and thus acted in the way she wanted her mother to have done.

Dora's reaction to her father's blend of visual impairment and scotomization was exhibitionistic. Her prominent fainting fits— besides addressing themselves to the visual field, where her father was both scotomized and traumatized—were regressive attempts to invert the role of her youth when she was the preferred nurse of her ill father. Her parents' stress on externals, from cleaning house to pretending the existence of a platonic relationship, triggered Dora's defensive lack of introspection, her spying on her father's comings and goings, and the exhibition of her sickened body. She attacked her father's vision, where he was weakest. If she could not force him to acknowledge his machinations, she fainted and thereby forced him to look at her desperate symptoms. Meanwhile, her parents continued to meet—unknowingly—at the site of her scarred mind and body.

4

What Was the Matter with Waking to Dreams?

At the end of the second session, when I expressed my satisfaction at the result, Dora replied in a deprecatory tone: "Why, has anything so very remarkable come out?"

Freud valued dreams for their avoidance of repression in dramatizing recent and childhood experiences (15). That feature, along with the convenience of textually manageable oneiric material, induced him to use Dora's two dreams as organizing set pieces in his narrative—a harbinger of the Wolf Man's case history. At every turn in the discussion to follow, we are confronted with uncertainties about psychoanalyst and patient as they grapple with the nocturnal narratives. What new meanings did Dora's first dream acquire when she dreamt it again during therapy and then when she told it? How did Freud's previous (mis)understanding of her traumatic life contribute to the dream's recurrence? How did Dora's trauma and first dream cumulatively influence Freud's interpretive stance? And, in turn, how did his (mis)interpretation of her traumatic life and first dream influence Dora in having her second dream and then telling it when she did? What stable answers can be found when we sift through the sum of Freud's clinical biases, his unempathic relationship with Dora, and his interpretive bullying and his forcing of her associations?

Freud's chapter on Dora's first dream falls into four sections. Their overlapping nature and logical looseness indicate some measure of his processive style. The sections constitute his analysis of the dream over a three-day period (64–74); the use of the dream to understand Dora's enuresis, leucorrhea, and masturbation (74–85); an objection to the theory of dreams (85–88); and a partial synthesis (88–93). Here is Freud's report of the first dream, followed by my fairly literal translation:

> In einem Haus brennt es, erzählte Dora, der Vater steht vor meinem Bett und weckt mich auf. Ich kleide mich schnell an. Die Mama will noch ihr Schmuckkästschen retten, der Papa sagt aber: Ich will nicht, dass ich und meine beiden Kinder wegen deines Schmuckkästschens verbrennen. Wir eilen herunter, und sowie ich draussen bin, wache ich auf. (G.W., 5:225)

> It's burning in a house, Dora recounted; Father is standing before my bed and wakes me up. I dress myself quickly. Mama, though, wants to save her jewel box, but Papa says: I don't want myself and both my children to be burnt up by fire because of your jewel box. We hurry downstairs, and as soon as I am outside, I wake up.[1]

And here is Strachey's translation:

> Here is the dream as related by Dora: 'A house was on fire. My father was standing beside my bed and woke me up. I dressed quickly. Mother wanted to stop and save her jewel-case; but Father said: 'I refuse to let myself and my two children be burnt for the sake of your jewel-case.' We hurried downstairs, and as soon as I was outside I woke up. (64)

Comparing the German and standard English versions enables us to uncover a number of textual subtleties that could be overlooked in a rapid reading. While sometimes trivial, the distortions found in the translation in the *Standard Edition* also involve such critical issues as Freud's grammar of dreams, the instability of paternal referents, the indefiniteness of the parental house ("*a* house"), and the acuteness of danger. Dora's whole dream takes place in the present tense, a grammatical form harmonizing with the hallucinatory nature of the oneiric material, which perforce occurs in the present. As I explained some years ago (1986b), the

---

1. See the interesting translation and commentary by C. Robins (1991). Compared with the translation in *S.E.*, the one by Robins is a decided improvement, although I disagree with much of his commentary.

pastness characterizing the English version of the dream flies in the face of the grammatical theory that Freud laid down for dreams. I should add here that Freud, but not Strachey, renders most of the associations in the main text and footnotes in the present tense; contrariwise, Freud puts the theoretical interruption of the clinical material mostly in the past tense (229–230/67–68), then dramatically resumes writing about the clinical material in the present tense. In the German text both the dream and the clinical associations with it are thus offered in the present, with the result that no abrupt grammatical marking occurs between primary and secondary process or between the initial time of Dora's dream and its subsequent elaboration in Freud's office.

Object relations constitute another difference between the German and English texts of the dream. The latter represents Dora as referring to her parents by the formal "Mother" and "Father." In the German text, the appellation for Philip shifts from "Father" to "Papa" at the very point when his rescuing role assumes greater urgency. Käthe's designation is the familiar "Mama," a lexical feature in keeping with Dora's behavioral identification with her mother for days on end before the dream (75). Note, too, that in the standard English translation Dora's father stands beside the bed, not in front of it. By using "beside," Strachey places Dora and her father closer than the German text permits.[2]

We may also observe that Dora did not assign the house an owner or a long-term resident; rather, she introduces it with the indefinite article, befitting the alienation of the loosely knit Bauer family. Significantly, once outside the perilous containment of the Bauer house, Dora wakes up. She makes no mention of the other family members being out of danger. The English version respects those nuances, but its first sentence, "A house was on fire," mistakenly leaves open the possibility that the whole house was ablaze. Whereas Strachey's rendering of this part of the manifest dream is more alarming than the German version, he diminishes the danger of being "burnt up by fire" into that of simply being "burnt."

2. *Er steht* (he stands) may also mean "his penis is erect" (Robins, 1991, 50).

Freud tries to track down the causes for both the first occurrence of the dream and its reappearance during treatment. For one thing, Philip expressed concern after noticing that the house at the lake was without a lightning rod and therefore could catch fire; fire, of course, is an element that figures in the dream symbolically as dangerous sexual passion. Proceeding with the dream analysis, Freud posits that Dora's dream at the lake did not happen immediately after the trauma but rather the next day, when the key to her bedroom door was missing. It was excited by her fear of sleeping in the unlocked room and having had to dress quickly. According to Freud, the dream expressed Dora's intention to get no rest until she left the lake house. It is curious, however, that Freud failed to consider as another precipitating cause of the dream the consultation that Dora had with him immediately before she and her father went to the lake. Dora had gone to visit Freud unwillingly, accompanied by her father. Was Freud's residence, even so early in the treatment, condensed into the image of the burning house in the dream? And wasn't Dora, too, afire with passion and rage? Freud traces a few causes for the reoccurrence of the dream during the treatment: a family argument over the dangers of fire, related to Käthe's locking her son in at night; Freud's interpretive use of the proverb "There can be no smoke without fire"; and Dora's transferential desire to kiss Freud, who, like her father and Hans, was a passionate smoker.[3] (This detail ties in to Dora's sensation of smelling smoke each time she awoke from her recurrent dream.) We can only conjecture about the deeper countertransferential meaning and transferential impact of Freud's maxim, which he repeated to Dora often (73).

A careful reading of Freud's text makes us aware of a series of sessional events that took place shortly before the dream and contributed to its reoccurrence: Freud informed Dora that she had revived her love for her father to protect herself against Hans;

3. Freud did not point out that Dora mistakenly placed her parents' other argument over the pearl drops four years earlier than her therapy, or one year before the dream. Four years earlier would mean two years before the dream (230/68; Strachey assigns the parenthetical remark "one year before the dream" to Freud, whereas the German text shows it as part of Dora's discourse).

Dora blamed her father for making her ill; she imitated her mother for many days; Freud pursued his inquiry about masturbation and leucorrhea; and Dora fingered her purse. An interpretive standoff ensued between Freud and Dora, he being oriented toward a masculine position and she being entrenched for some days in a identifying with her mother and blaming the male. Freud, caught up in his reconstruction of the past, interpreted Dora's fingering of the reticule as masturbatory and related it to early bedwetting, but he overlooked such meanings as the current fear of seducing, the wish to be, and fear of being, seduced, and the wish to be rescued. But we may ask, Did the purse stand for the jewel that she received from her father through the agency of Peppina and that looked like the one carried by the latter? Pushed by her own deepest homosexual current, was Dora masturbating Peppina or someone else, perhaps even *inside* her own vagina?[4] Did Dora project her conflict about staying in the burning house onto her dilatory mother?

Freud had been gratified by the Dora's "readiness" to convey part of her pathogenic material, yet by the time of the first dream mutual dissatisfaction had apparently begun to replace gratification. Freud evinced fidelity in his empathy with Hans, first in the latter's erotic designs and then in his sexual frustration. For Freud, the main thrust of Dora's dream was in her erotic strivings, aimed at her father not as a primary but rather as a defensively regressive choice—hence her effort to replace her repressed love of Hans with her love for her protective father, that is, "her flight from life into disease" (122).

Although the dream recurred during the treatment, its transferential significance may have been not only "new" (as Freud would have it, 93) but also dominant. We might question, for example, whether the indefinite house carried accrued transferential meanings concerning the danger that both Dora's body and Freud's consulting room were ablaze. We may also wonder

---

4. See especially 70, 75, 76, 78. For Krohn and Krohn (1982) the parapraxis signifies the sexual penetration of another woman.

whether Freud appeared as both parents in her dream—as the father, seen ambivalently as one who awakens into self-examination and as one from whom she has to flee in order to wake up and find the aloneness of her safety; and as the self-engrossed analytic mother who is interested primarily not in others but in the safety of the jewel box, encasing sexual theories. For Dora's idea that the mystery of her dream turns upon her mother, Freud offers merely oedipal jealousy (70, 90).

The struggle between Freud and Dora primed both of them and informed a symptomatic act that she carried out before narrating her dream. When Freud went to fetch Dora from the waiting room, she hurriedly concealed a letter that she was reading. At first she refused Freud's request to know who the sender was; later it was identified as her grandmother begging Dora to write more often. Freud concludes that the withheld information "was a matter of complete indifference and had no relation to the treatment"; Dora wanted just "to play 'secrets'" with him. In contrast to Freud, we may at least consider whether she felt uneasy in recounting how a grandmotherly figure cared for her, whether the envelope of the letter resembled the symbolic jewel box, whether a woman, by virtue of her letter, was inside it, whether Dora was again engaging in an act of sexual fingering, and whether she was hiding her "private" matters from a contaminating male (78).

Freud's clinical manner was symptomatically directive. After narrating her dream Dora tried to free-associate: "Something occurs to me but it cannot belong to the dream, for it is quite recent." Not allowing Dora to proceed freely, Freud told her that the event would belong to the dream, and urged her to continue, assuring her that her association would be "the most recent thing" fitting in with the dream (65; compare 93).[5] Upon hearing about a dispute in the Bauer family, Freud went on to interpret that in the lake scene Dora wanted to give her jewel case to Hans but feared

5. For other comments about Freud's prevention of Dora's free associations, see Kanzer, 1980, 75, 79.

him and, even more, herself.[6] We then read: "Naturally Dora
would not follow me in this part of the interpretation." To us,
bearing in mind Freud's marital plans for Dora, which excluded
the engineer whom he thought was courting her, and Freud's
fantasy of her unbefitting reaction at the lake, the word "naturally" carries a cold irony. At the end of that first session devoted to
the dream, Freud corralled Dora's associative processes by keeping her in anticipation, promising to go beyond his interpretation
that Dora feared her love of Hans.

Opening up his description of the next hour, Freud shows us
how his theory of sexuality is itself sexualized. His metaphor of a
dream as a corporeal shape positioned on two legs, one leg standing in childhood and the other in the present (71), links up with a
suggestive Viennese gesture at the time: two outstretched fingers,
signifying either "eleven" or "a pair of legs" (Freud, 1974, 323).
From that sexualized description, the reader passes to Freud's
account of the session, at which Freud performed a countertransferential gesture that, escaping his comprehension, belied his very
boast that the session was "as usual, successful." It was a symptomatic act that imitated Dora's symptomatic acts, continued the
harassing, directive nature of his interpretations, and showed him
behaving once again like Hans. To catch Dora, Freud bade her
turn around to see if there was anything special about his table, on which there was a newly placed match-holder (*Behälter*,
233/71, translated as "match-stand" in *S.E.*). Owing to the impress of Freud's smoking and his recurrent interpretive use of the
proverb "There can be no smoke without fire," the match-holder
continued highly charged, ambivalent fantasies, however asym-
metrically shared between Freud and Dora. We might go even
further: because the purse fingering occurred shortly before the
dream session and because, indeed, Dora began the dream session
by hiding the letter (78), we might say that Freud's experiment

6. At this juncture *S.E.* offers an erroneous translation. Referring to Dora's
dispute concerning the danger of locking Otto in his bedroom every night, Freud
asks: "They [sie] related that to the danger of fire?"; compare *S.E.*: "And that made
you think of the risk of fire?" (226/65).

with the match-holder on the following day continued the fantasy of holding or containment peculiar to the symptomatic acts.[7] When Dora said that she had not noticed the match-holder he had purposefully placed on the desk, Freud condescendingly asked her if she knew why children are not allowed to play with matches. Not getting the answer he wanted, he alluded to the folk belief that children wet their bed if they play with fire; and he lectured her on the link between matches, fire, water, and bedwetting. Freud's own association prompted him to synonymize the antithesis fire–water, such that sexual passion involves sexual wetness. In brief, the pressure of Freud's interpretations was relentless, and Dora might have been transferentially alluding to her clinical imprisonment when she recalled that her brother was locked in his room at night. It is not clear, however, whether Freud shared two other interpretations with Dora: that water also alludes to vaginal catarrh and "drops" and that the latter switch word (a mnemonic trace of Philip's gift of pearl drops, rejected by Käthe in an unforgettable marital argument) also refers to the jewel box (*Schmuckkästschen*, 254/92), a symbol of intact female genitals and the dream's most condensed and displaced element. Strachey (91n) pertinently underscores that *Schmuck* denotes ornaments and decorations of all kinds and that as an adjective it can mean "tidy" and "neat."

An unremitting brightness pervades Freud's German chapter on Dora's first dream: his commentary on the theme of waking. The commentary is unfortunately hidden in the English translation. The German for "wake" is the irregular verb *wecken* (to wake), and its cognates *erwecken, aufwecken,* and *wachrufen* resurface in their literal and metaphorical meanings throughout the case history. Also embedded in the German text is the kindred idea that sleeping appears in various guises throughout one's waking life (compare Mahony, 1989, chap. 3).

In the first dream Philip is pictured as waking (*weckt auf*) his

---

7. Langs (1980, 66) wrongly believes that Freud's symptomatic act preceded the two by Dora; just the opposite happened.

daughter up, and as Dora reaches the outside of the house she literally wakes up (*wache auf*).[8] *Wecken* occurs much more frequently in Freud's interpretative commentary than in his narrative of the dream. Collapsing metalanguage into language, Freud states that a recurrent dream by its very nature is particularly likely to "wake up" (*wecken*, 225/64) his curiosity. In *The Interpretation of Dreams* he had already focused on the relation between waking thoughts (*Wachgedanken*) and the "unconscious wish which forms the dream" (249/87). He realizes, however, that by conceiving dreams as the representation of unconscious wishes, he has aroused (*wachgerufen*, 230/68) his readers' inclination to contradict.

The wish creating the dream serves to wake up (*erwecken*, 233/71) childhood to reality. Besides that, Dora's dream was a reaction to a recent experience that itself summoned or woke up (*wecken*, 254/92) her only previous analogous experience. More precisely, the dream drew on her memory of being woken up (*weckt*, 234/72) by Hans at the lake house and stirred up (*wachrufen*, 232/70 and 249/86) her old love for her father as a protector; supposedly, he used to wake her up (*weckte*, 252/89) as a child so that she would not wet the bed. Both in the dream and in waking reality, then, Dora stirred up (*wachgerufen*, 249/86) her infantile love of her father in order to keep her love of Hans repressed. Dora also had a belated memory of waking up (*Erwachen*, 235/73) after the dream each time and smelling smoke. The smell persisted past her waking (*Erwachen*, 254/92) and revived (*aufgeweckt*, 236/74) her memory of being kissed at the shop by Hans, a smoker.

Lastly, there remains the possible connection between Dora's dream occurring on three nights by the lake and Freud's specific

8. Freud mentions in chapter 1 that early in life Dora's critical powers were "awakened" (*erwachte*; cf. *S.E.*, "developed"—176/18). Freud uses the key verb just a few times in the commentary on the second dream: Hans's advances "aroused" (*wachgerufen*, 269/106) fresh emotions in Dora; among those emotions was an "awakened" jealousy (*geweckten*, 273/109); Freud declares his aim is to "wake up" (*aufweckt*, 272/109) the most evil demons living in the human breast.

analysis of it—according to his report—over three sessions (71, 73). "Times and dates," Freud insists elsewhere about other issues, "were never without significance for her" (120). Did the analysis of the first dream take three days, or, very likely, did Freud confine the report of its analysis to a three-day period? Was this an unconscious time awareness on his part? Although the dream alludes to Dora's wish to leave treatment, she waited until she had her second dream to announce her departure. In an anniversary reaction, might Dora have telescoped her first dream and its dramatic reappearances into the three remaining days of treatment? And might she have had some faint awareness in linking her departure from the lake and later her abandonment of treatment? Because the end of the dream is specific about Dora's safety but not about that of other family members, did her guilt about surviving or guilt about intended activities prevent her from continuing the dream? These questions beckon us to consider other temporal issues involved in the next dream and the end of the treatment.

There are several indications that during the final phase of therapy Dora became increasingly febrile. Her decision to quit therapy arose two weeks prior to its end. Next, she wondered why she had kept the lake trauma to herself and suddenly let her mother know. Freud, for his part, thought that Dora's hurt feelings needed explanation, especially since he was beginning to consider Hans's overtures as seriously intended. Meanwhile, as we learn from a neglected retrospective account of the Dora case that Freud committed to paper in 1914, his insistent quest for details of the lake scene was reaching a crescendo: "I had knowledge of the scene which occasioned the outbreak of the current illness. I tried innumerable times to submit this experience to analysis, but even direct demands always failed to produce from her anything more than the same meager and incomplete description of it. Not until a long détour, leading back over her earliest childhood, had been made, did a dream present itself" (1914, 10). In this connection let me note that Dora's dream fulfilled not only her own wish but also Freud's and gave him some "desired" confirmation.[9] And the confirmation that Freud hankered for concerned his *previous* assumption that Dora's second trauma had given rise to her fantasy of defloration (94, 104).

Compared to the overlapping trifold examination of the first dream, the partitioned exposition of the succeeding dream seems to be more clearly defined: two days of dream analysis are mixed together, a third day is presented, and then comes posttreatment reflection and a synthesis of the case. Freud's report of Dora's dream reads this way in German (for ease of reading, I have dropped the italics in the original and the following translations):

> Ich gehe in einer Stadt, die ich nicht kenne, spazieren, sehe Strassen und Plätze, die mir fremd sind. Ich komme dann in ein Haus, wo ich wohne, gehe auf mein Zimmer und finde dort einen Brief der Mama liegen. Sie schreibt: Da ich ohne Wissen der Eltern vom Hause fort bin, wollte sie mir nicht schreiben, dass der Papa erkrankt ist. Jetzt ist er gestorben, und wenn Du willst, kannst Du kommen. Ich gehe nun zum Bahnhofe und frage etwa 100mal: Wo ist der Bahnhof? Ich bekomme immer die Antwort: Fünf Minuten. Ich sehe dann einen dichten Wald vor mir, in den ich hineingehe, und frage dort einen Mann, dem ich begegne. Er sagt mir: Noch 2½ Stunden. Er bietet mir an, mich zu begleiten. Ich lehne ab und gehe allein. Ich sehe den Bahnhof vor mir und kann ihn nicht erreichen. Dabei ist das gewöhnliche Angstgefühl, wenn man im Traume nicht weiter kommt. Dann bin ich zu Hause, dazwischen muss ich gefahren sein, davon weiss ich aber nichts.—Trete in die Portierloge und frage ihn nach unserer Wohnung. Das Dienstmädchen öffnet mir und antwortet: Die Mama und die anderen sind schon auf dem Friedhofe. (*G.W.*, 5:256–257)

Here is my translation:

---

9. "Desired" for *erwünschte* (256/94); compare Strachey's "desirable," which wrongly leaves open the possibility that the desire for confirmation was realized *after* the fact.

I go walking in a city that I do not know, and I see streets and squares that are strange to me. Then I come into a house where I live, go to my room, and find Mama's letter lying there. She writes: Since I [Dora] am away from home without my parents' knowledge, she didn't wish to write to me that Papa took ill. Now he has died, and if you [Dora] want, you can come. So I go to the station and ask perhaps 100 times: Where is the station? I always receive the answer: Five minutes. Then I see a thick wood in front of me and I go into it and ask a man whom I meet there. He says to me: 2½ hours more. He offers to accompany me. I refuse and go alone. I see the station in front of me and cannot reach it. At the same time I have the usual feeling of anxiety that one gets when one cannot go farther in a dream. Then I am home; in the meantime I must have traveled but I know nothing about that.—I step into the porter's lodge and ask him about our apartment. The maidservant opens for me and replies: Your mom and the others are already at the cemetery.

A charged complex of chronological factors affected the dream and its analysis. Because only three sessions were devoted to the dream and because, as Freud said, the last day of treatment was December 31, 1900 (a Monday), Dora must have told Freud her dream on Friday and seen him on his next usual working day, Saturday, and then on the final Monday. Freud presents the clinical material of the first two days mixed together, except for two addenda to the dream specifically assigned to the second day. The addenda read: *"I see myself particularly distinctly going up the stairs"* and *"After her answer I go to my room, but not at all sadly, and begin reading a big book that lies on my writing-table"* (256n/94n, my translation). The additions elaborate on Dora's activities in the dream when she returned home for the second, enjoyable time (as opposed to the first time, when she returned home and read her mother's accusatory letter mentioning her husband's death). Significantly, Dora did not remember those points when she first reported the dream on Friday—which was also the day when family members had to leave the house because of Käthe's fanatical cleaning. I submit that having to wait until Saturday before she could freely stay at home overdetermined Dora's recall of the added points.[10] I also suggest that Dora's dream might be one of those whose content anticipates the way patients will communicate them. If so, the time that it took Dora to walk to the station in her dream was replicated by her telling the dream halfway into the session, thereby leaving two and a half hours to go in her treatment.[11]

To further my analysis, I shall first examine Dora's dream in Strachey's translation, which has had such a determining impact on Anglo-American readers:

> I was walking about in a town which I did not know. I saw streets and squares which were strange to me. Then I came into a house where I lived, went to my room, and found a letter from Mother lying there. She wrote saying that as I had left home without my parents' knowledge she had not wished to write to me to say that Father was ill. "Now he is dead, and if you like you can come." I then went to the station and asked about a hundred times: "Where is the station?" I always got the answer: "Five minutes." I then saw a thick wood before me which I went into, and there I asked a man whom I met. He said to me: "Two and a half hours more." He offered to accompany me. But I refused and went alone. I saw the station in front of me and could not reach it. At the same time I had the usual feeling of anxiety that one has in dreams when one cannot move forward. Then I was at home. I must have been travelling in the meantime, but I know nothing about that. I walked into the porter's lodge, and enquired for our flat. The maidservant opened the door to me and replied that Mother and the others were already at the cemetery. (94)

Among the several shortcomings in the translation in the

10. On Fridays and other occasions when Käthe cleaned house, all the family members were obliged to leave the apartment (Rogów, 1978, 343).

11. McCaffrey (1984, 85) observes that the two and a half hours mentioned in the dream may be a telescoped anniversary of the two and a half years between the lake incident and the final days of treatment.

Standard Edition, let me mention four. They indicate the influence of Strachey's defensiveness and censorship upon his translation. First, as usual, Strachey carries out a temporal displacement by translating the present tense of the dream into the past. In doing so, he repeatedly violates Freud's grammatical theory of dreams. Second, Strachey has again formalized the intimate references to Dora's mother and father. Third, Strachey arbitrarily edits through the use of clarifying punctuation. On four occasions in the *Standard Edition* we notice quotation marks used to set off the message in Käthe's letter and the dialogue between Dora and her interlocutors. Freud, however, uses no such punctuation; he thereby bypasses clarity in favor of a pronounced primary process, which creates a flow and thrust toward condensation in his textuality.

Fourth, to some extent, Strachey desexualizes the lexicality. He adds the word "door" after "open": "The maidservant opened the door to me." The omission of "door" in the German renders the maid's action more sexually ambiguous. As Freud comments about Dora's first dream: "The question whether a woman is 'open' or 'shut' can naturally not be a matter of indifference" (67n). In discussing the second dream, however, Freud does not go into this textual ambiguity concerning Dora's same-sex feelings.

The other instance of desexualization concerns the verbs "go" and "come," which occur in Dora's dream and her two addenda occur ten times, sometimes in alternate succession. Once, moreover, the German *kommen* is echoed in the verb *bekomme* (answer). Such an extraordinary textual element, muted in the English version, justifies extracting the lexical items from their syntactical context and seeing in them a condensed latent plot: like the English "come," the German *kommen* colloquially refers to orgasm; on the other hand, *gehen* (go) is commonly used in both languages to mean "urinate" or "defecate."[12]

---

12. For this observation I am indebted to Robins (1991, 59, 69). Strachey

Dora's two dreams are complementary. As suggested by my remarks on the English translation, the second dream has more primary process elements and a more complex libidinality. Additionally, the father-protector in Dora's first dream emerges as the paternal victim of her vengeance in the second. In both dreams Dora cannot be at home safe with her parents; at the end of the first, however, she is alone outside the house, whereas in the second dream she is essentially alone, inside and outside. The theme of safety and isolation is dramatized more forcefully in a series of contradictory statements distinguishing the second dream.[13] Being lost in space is hence emblematic of Dora's inner disorientation as she walks about in a town strange to her: she goes to *a* house (indefinite, as in the first dream) where she lives; she goes to the station and asks repeatedly, "Where is the station?"; she is told first "five minutes" and later "two and a half hours more"; she goes to the porter's lodge and asks about her apartment. It is only at the end of the dream, reported in an addendum, that she feels at home—reading a big book while others are at the cemetery. Assuming her mother's position, she has now cleaned everyone out of her house.

In analyzing the first dream, Freud focuses to a large extent on relating Dora's lakeside trauma to her childhood, whereas in analyzing the second he concentrates nearly exclusively on relating the lakeside trauma to her recent past. Thus, during the first two days in analyzing the dream, Freud felt enlightened about her symptom of appendicitis and received confirmation of his assumption regarding her fantasy of defloration. But on the third day, Dora began by saying that the session was her last—news that came like the shock of dry thunder. Freud, kindled rather than kind, charged ahead and tried to make the most of the remaining hour of treatment.

---

(257) mutes the libidinal flooding that distinguishes the German text. Freud does not address this textual feature, which in various guises often shows up in dreams when a patient reacts intensely to the therapeutic process.

13. Compare Lewin, 1973, 526: "Dora, following her self-exile from her family at the end of the first dream, is now completely alienated from them."

For at least four or five weeks after her therapy ended (121), Dora was in a state of befuddlement. Freud also felt befuddled, but in his own way. That reaction manifested itself not only in his memory of the treatment of Dora's dream but also in his significant commentary on it. Thus, in an uncanny parallel to his theoretical stand that dreams clarify dreamers' symptoms and fill gaps in their amnesias, Freud's reactions included a symptomatic enactment regarding Dora's first dream and amnesia regarding her second.

In particular, while stating that for Dora stopping treatment was tangled up with the content of her dream, Freud reveals that the aborted treatment affected his memory and his capacity to reproduce its most recent material: "In consequence of the peculiar circumstances amidst which we broke off—circumstances bound up with the [dream] content—everything was not cleared up. *And also connected with this* is that my memory has not retained the sequence of my conclusions with equal certainty at every point. . . . I shall therefore bring forward the material produced for the analysis of this dream, in the almost confused order that it comes in my active memory" (*G.W.*, 257, my translation and italics).[14] Thereupon Freud proceeds, as if in his own dream, to present the clinical material "in the somewhat haphazard order" in which it recurred to his mind. His groping, dispersed, and somewhat confused commentary on the defensive layering of Dora's dream fantasies may be clarified in this way. He found two situations in the dream. The first contains three layered fantasies: of revenge, of defloration, and (the most important) of waiting for a fiancé. More specifically, the facade of the first situation consists of a fantasy of revenge against the father; behind that fantasy lies concealed the fantasy of revenge against Hans; the latter fantasy in turn screens tender fantasies involving happy anticipation, defloration by Hans, and childbirth.

The triple-tiered fantasies informing the first situation hide

14. The translation in *S.E.* (95) is not so harsh about Freud's memory: "I am not equally certain at every point of the order in which my conclusions were reached."

the second situation, which involves Dora's love for Peppina and, once again, fantasies of defloration, although this time Dora identifies with the male agent in erotic quest. According to Freud, in reproducing the second situation of her dream, Dora forgot to ask: "Does Herr ——— live here?" and "Where does Herr ——— live?" With suggestive reticence, Freud states that Dora's forgetting those questions stemmed from their charged reference to her patrilineal surname. If we further consider that in Viennese dialect at the turn of the century, *Bauer* was slang for "sperm," we recognize even more the prevalence of Dora's masculine identification in the second situation.[15] Note that Freud never discussed with Dora the second situation of her dream; because he became aware of her homosexual strivings after the therapy, he analyzed with her only her feelings of heterosexual vengeance and love. Let us also not forget that at the end of the chapter on the dream Freud returned to the second situation and once more tried to lessen the confusion of his explanation. After telling us that the remaining third and fourth lowest levels of Dora's psychic life are her love for Hans and Peppina, Freud ends with the free-floating comment: "Cruel and sadistic tendencies find satisfaction in this dream" (111n)

A motif of containment is discernible in the Dora case and, for that matter, in many of Freud's other clinical and expository writings. Components of that motif are openings and closings and such variants as receptacles and keys. References to that which can be opened, Freud again and again stresses, lend themselves to being interpreted to indicate the act of penetrating a woman. We read that such words as "box," "case," "chest," and "cupboard" symbolize the uterus (1900, 354; 1901, 49–52; and 1913, 292); the German word for receptacle, *Büsche*, vulgarly denotes the

---

15. *Baublods* was a dialectic word for the female genitalia; see the appendix on erotic slang in the modern edition of *Josefine Mutzenbacher* (1985, 187, 200–201, 223). Freud adds that there was a similar play on the aunt's name and the visit to the cemetery. Perhaps he had in mind the play between the aunt's name (Friedmann), cemetery (*Friedhof*), and "to copulate with the devil" (*friedhofieren*); see the entries at 33.1 and 33.2 in Ernest Borneman's erotic lexicon (1984).

female genitals (1900, 154). On several occasions Freud points out the relevant verbal play in *Schrank* (cabinet), *Schranke* (barrier or enclosure), *einschränken* (to restrict), and *eingeschränkt* (confined, narrow-minded; Nunberg and Federn, 1967, 80 and 30n; also Freud, 1900, 407; Freud, 1915–16, 121). In this connection we might note that the impact of Freud's childhood experience concerning his absent mother and nanny was overdetermined by the interacting words *Kasten* (wardrobe, box) and *einkasteln* (to box, to lock up—Freud, 1985, 271–272).

The thematic terms of containment and closure as opposed to escape illustrate Dora's plight. Käthe wanted Dora to submit to domestic containment, whereas Philip and the Zellenka couple wanted to enclose her in their erotic circuit. In her two traumas, Dora wrenched herself out of Hans's entrapment and ran away from him. In terms of a problematic containment, her dreams form a sequence. She first escaped from a burning house and then finally managed to return home after her family members had left. At the end of the first dream she is outside. Then, magically, she wanders far away, to a strange town, only to learn that in the meantime her father has died. She returns to the enclosure of her home and is alone—at home and not at home—for the others are at the cemetery. We might speculate as to Dora's third dream. Would she have dreamt of a dream on fire? or that she was inside or outside the dream?

Many decisive events and influences marked Dora's life, including her traumas and her marginalization as a Jew, a female, and, for a span, an adolescent. However great their impact, they cannot be called exceptional in light of the unfortunate historical fact that many of Dora's peers had similarly terrible lives. The most spectacular element in Dora's whole case history was the equally spectacular desire on Dora's part for good containment—her alleged two-hour meditation before Raphael's painting of the Madonna embracing a child.[16] Given the constraints imposed on an

---

16. Briefly inspecting the same picture in 1883, Freud thought that Raphael's subject resembled a young nursemaid more than it did a Madonna: Raphael's

adolescent girl visiting a museum alone in a distant city in the nineteenth century and given the developmental constraints with respect to a youth's prolonged response to an aesthetic object, the credibility of Dora's meditation feat increases the later we place it after her second trauma and the closer to her troubling therapy. This said, I nevertheless doubt the reported duration of that experience, and I am amazed that Freud, otherwise so skeptical of his patient, did not question the temporality of her account. For my part, I have never met a historian of art or a psychoanalyst who claimed to have gazed at a painting for two hours, unless for the purpose of lecturing or publishing a study.

Whatever the length of Dora's meditative watch, it manifested her longing for maternal love. Although she later tried to liberate herself by reading and by attending feminist conferences, she never grew up and remained a wounded child, lost in place and time. For a decade she resided in Merano, which was under the pervasive influence of Tyrolean Catholicism and its Marian cult, which bordered on heretical adoration.[17] As a visitor to the

---

Madonna "is a girl, say 16 years old; she gazes out on the world with such a fresh and innocent expression, half against my will she suggested to me a charming, sympathetic nursemaid, not from the celestial world but from ours. My Viennese friends reject this opinion of mine as heresy and refer to a superb feature round the eyes making her a Madonna" (Freud, 1960, 97).

17. Compare Blum's (1994, 529–530) hasty conclusions: "The evidence suggests that the fantasy of and identification with the Christian mother, the Virgin Mary, long preceded her [Dora's] marriage. . . . The material was overdetermined and probably also referred to Dora's desire to leave her Jewish analyst, parents, and heritage for the idealized Christian mother with whom she identified." I would say rather that the Sistina experience points to Dora's womanly ideal; to claim that she identified with the Christian representation of that ideal is another issue. As a matter of fact, Dora converted to Protestantism, which, in contrast to Catholicism and even more to Tyrolean Catholicism, is characterized by the absence of any Marian cult. That cult was abundantly manifested in open-air shrines (one of which still stands next to the church of Saint Nicolaus), public statuary, and processions with pictorial banners. The procession that Dora was to have seen would have occurred between the church of Saint Nicolaus in the Domplatz and the nearby Sandplatz, a square that was much more important in Merano history at the end of the nineteenth century. The Sandplatz was dominated by an imposing statue, erected in 1801, of the Virgin Mother, guardian of the Tyroleans against their enemies.

Dresden museum, Dora carried with her some impressions of the Tyrolean cult honoring an ideal, protective mother. The figures in the Holy Family overdetermined Dora's homosexual desire for Peppina; let us remark that the shortened form of Giuseppina (Josephina) was itself the feminized form of Joseph, the name of Jesus' foster father. Perhaps Dora imagined that to be held as the Christ child was held by the Madonna would restore her and would counteract Hans's traumatic clasp. Accordingly, if only in a retrospective sense, Dora's two-hour meditative watch in the museum served as an anniversary phenomenon neutralizing her two-hour flight from Hans.

Shortly after meeting Dora, Freud wrote to Fliess that her case "has smoothly opened to the existing collection of picklocks" (1985, 427). In a similar statement at the end of the case history itself, Freud proclaims: "No one who disdains the key [of sexuality] will ever be able to unlock the door" (278/115).[18] A symbolic key with the power to open takes on far-reaching import (compare 67n and 91) when the door is Dora's body or, more exactly, her symbolic *Schmuckkästschen,* or "genitals"; Freud's own symptomatic use of the match holder symbolically referred to the female genitals containing the penis. Paradoxically, then, Freud had to open her up in order to contain her. And he sought to undo Dora's self-containment while he struggled against containment or confinement himself. He boasted that whereas no one so far "confined" (*einschränken,* 270/115) the scope of his sexual claims, he himself had to contend with social restrictions (*Einschränkungen,* 165/9).

In the clinical drama that followed, Dora expressed doubts and questions in order to break the closure of Freud's interpretations. He tried to immure her in his theories, in his interpretive

18. As if anticipating his conception of antithetic primal language, Freud counterbalances his ameliorative use of "key" (*Schlüssel*) with a pejorative one, expressed in the thought that his prurient readers would use his case history as a "roman á clef" (*Schlüsselroman,* 165/9. Note that German cognates of *Schlüssel* are *Aufschluss* (solution) and *schliessen* (to shut up, to conclude). In his suggestive footnote (18½₃) Freud refers to Dora's "shutting [her letter] away" (*eingeschlossen*), supplies his "solution" (*Aufschluss*) and "concludes" (*schliesse*).

constructions of reversing symbols, turning her nos into yeses, and reading her reproaches as self-reproaches. It was tragic that Freud, hell-bent on turning Dora's statements against her, did not explore the source of his own hostility toward her. The letter that Dora tried to conceal from him and that he held to be simply an instrument in a game of secrets might also have been her manifestation of self-containment and a transferential protest against his hostile intrusiveness. With loaded purposes she brought into her sessions with him oneiric material of flight and fighting enclosure.

The second dream became an organizing experience for Freud and Dora in their tug-of-war. Their stimulation and frustration of each other provoked mutual impatience—on Freud's part, for Dora to yield her secrets, and on Dora's part, for Freud to manifest more personal interest. Yet that contrast is too simple. The evidence at our disposal makes it impossible to pinpoint the shifting, relative power of the ambivalent wishes of both parties, whose interaction was multilayered, evolving, and asymmetrical. A manifold ambivalence prevailed; they each wished to overpower the other, to seduce and be seduced, to dislike the other and yet stay, to seduce and stay, to seduce and leave, to leave unless seduced or rescued, to cause departure as a defense against wanting to seduce.[19] For all Dora's libidinal turmoil, her dream enticed Freud to impress her. Fighting off his resolute pressure, she was subjected to his unbuttoned pique. Then she egged him on, she bearded him, he treated her amiss.

Rather than being free to associate to the dream's very first segment, Dora had to contend with Freud's immediate and intrusive guess about it. The segment in question, reworded in Freud's commentary, reads: "*She wanders alone in a strange town, and sees streets and squares.* She declares that it was certainly not B——, which I first guessed, but a town in which she was" (258/95, my translation). On the one hand, it is ironic that Freud avowedly delayed giving transferential interpretations and that, on the other

---

19. Compare Langs (1980, 65–66), who says that in reporting the second dream "Dora was attempting to save her analysis at the very juncture that she was thinking of abandoning it."

hand—given the important theme of postponement that he finds in the dream and lays at his patient's door—he impatiently gives interpretations from the outset. As if blinded by his hyperidentification with Hans, Freud engages in interpretive impetuosity, which resembles Hans's sexual impetuosity. The therapeutic dyad seems enmeshed in waiting and its performative variants—patience and delay, impatience and haste. Dora delays to talk about the lakeside trauma and waits to tell Freud about leaving, and he precipitously pursues his theoretical quest.

In his conflictual imbroglio with Dora, Freud trips over himself, calling her now a girl, now a child. When he reflects on her reading, he classifies Dora with fearful children: "Now children never read about forbidden subjects in an encyclopaedia *calmly*. They do it in fear and trembling, with an uneasy look over their shoulder to see if someone may not be coming" (263/100).[20] But when he talks about the lakeside seduction scene, he graduates her from childhood to girlhood, maintaining that a "normal girl" (95) would have not told her parents but would have kept Hans's amorous intention to herself. Accordingly, in the fluctuating descriptions of Dora, the rhetorical aim of the moment decides Freud's choice from among developmental designations.

Freud's dislike of Dora in the final days of treatment comes through in his ridicule, evident in the German text. When Dora dismissed Freud's attention to the detail of her going upstairs in the dream, he summoned up his verbal genius and fired back: "It was easy to brush aside this objection . . . by pointing out that if she had been able to travel in her dream from the unknown town to Vienna without making [*übergehen*] a railway journey she ought also to have been able to leave out [*sich hinwegsetzen*] a flight of stairs" (264/101). Strachey's translation of the verb *übergehen* as "without making" leaves out its literal locomotive meaning, "to skip over," which ironically also applies to going upstairs. Likewise, Strachey's translation of the verb *sich hinwegsetzen* as "leaving out" drops its literal meaning, "to leap, to jump over." In

20. Although I use *S.E.* here, I have silently changed its translation of *jemand* from "some one" to "someone."

sum, Freud revolves his condensed satire around two verbs whose literal meanings are "to skip" or "to jump over." Upon hearing Dora's literalistic conception of going up a flight of stairs in her dream Freud offers a comment whose contradictory ambiguity reflects the very essence of dreaming. In the same movement of verbal economy Freud both joins Dora and derides her.

In a second example we find again an unempathic Freud: "You will agree that nothing makes you so angry as having it thought that you merely fancied [*einbildet*] the scene by the lake. I know now—and this is what you do not want to be reminded of—that you *did* fancy [*sich engebildet*] that Herr K.'s proposals were serious, and that he would not leave off until you married him" (271–272/108). Freud uses the verb "fancy" (*einbilden*) in different ways, the first in the sense of deluding, the second in the sense of imagining. Exploiting an ambiguity, Freud puts into the same associative area two mentational processes that the beleaguered Dora strove to separate.[21] In this instance we see Freud parading his verbal dexterity at Dora's expense.

Never letting up on his story of impressive interconnections, Freud disallowed Dora sufficient analytic space and tried to force her associations to the dream in order to arrive at desired conclusions. Because analysts have for decades have been more impressed than Dora by Freud's seemingly tight narrative, a closer look at his inferences is called for. Freud's rapid reversal of dream images has a dazzling effect, but narrative coherence does not necessarily entail a correspondence to reality. For a case in point, we might review how Freud conceived of Dora's alleged fantasies of defloration and pregnancy and connected them to her symptoms of appendicitis and limping. Dora is reported to have said that her appendicitis occurred "nine months" after the lake scene. Let us set aside the fact that the date of the lake scene was June 30,

---

21. For the observations on the latter passage, I am indebted to Masson (1988, 56). I would simply add that in the last days of treatment Freud's verbal play with *einbilden* revolving around *Bild* (picture) is overdetermined. Freud relates the family pictures and those in the Dresden museum and Secessionist exhibition to *Weibsbild*, a derogatory term for a woman (99n).

that Dora's aunt died the following April 7, and that the appendicitis came "shortly after" (101), that is, at the earliest, in the tenth month after the aunt's death. Let us set aside the fact that even though Dora's family were not religious Jews, the big book that she calmly read in the dream might have been a Bible and not the sexually informative encyclopedia that Freud supposed it to be. Let us also set aside the fact that he does not bring in any evidence of earlier symptoms, such as cessation of menses or morning sickness, that might have reinforced his interpretation that dragging the foot was "a true hysterical symptom" (102) related to her fantasied pregnancy.

But we shall not set aside other objections. The encyclopedia that Dora could have consulted at the time did not contain the word *Vorhof* (vestibule of the vagina) but cursorily mentioned *Nymphae*, medical terms for the female genitalia that were not used by Dora but were inferred from the dream by Freud. To demonstrate Dora's defloration fantasies, Freud offers his own conclusion: some of Dora's words reminded *him* of *Vorhof* and *Nymphae*; therefore, the book she was reading at the end of her dream must have been an encyclopedia. Freud does not give any evidence that these technical terms are Dora's.[22] The extant evidence indicates that these terms are his own, in which case Freud was eroticizing his own language. Accordingly, in spite of his conscious denial, his dry technical language was not just eroticized but seductive.

22. Stadlen (1989) researched the various *Konversationslexika* that Dora might have consulted to find out about appendicitis in 1899. He cites two London medical specialists as sources for his diagnostic information and stresses that (1) all too shortly after the seven-year-old Dora injured her right foot and was laid up for several weeks, she went on an arduous mountain trip that could have caused permanent damage; (2) neither Freud nor Deutsch took that possibility into their diagnostic account, their belief being that Dora's lameness was a hysterical symptom that bore the meaning of making a "false step" (103); (3) a pain in the right leg (psoas spasm) is used as a diagnostic test for pelvic appendicitis; and localized inflammation would have been sufficient, without prior physical leg injury, to cause a dragging of the right foot. I would add that Dora's claudication, whatever its origin, might also have been influenced by her identification with Peppina, who, because she could not walk, had to spend several months in an asylum (33).

Freud was also like a detective and a prosecuting lawyer, aiming to find Dora out rather than to help her find herself. His portrayal of her as willful prevented him from seeing how she was grappling with the attitude of the adults around her and how in some ways she identified with them in their behavior of denial. A contrary problem is evident in Freud's overeagerness to interpret Dora's nonverbal reactions as consent. Thus, insisting on Dora's perduring love for Hans, Freud interpreted that Dora had defloration and childbirth fantasies; then he added, tooting his own horn, "And Dora disputed the fact no longer." We may question whether her silence is a confirmation of Freud's position. When he ventured to show his pride over his fathered interpretation, she made sure it was stillborn: "Why, has anything so very remarkable come out [herausgekommen]?"[23]

Let us next examine Freud's handling of the all-important lakeside incident in terms of his reportorial and interpretative reliability. In light of the fact that there are a series of lies in Freud's description of the Rat Man case (1987) and two lies in the "Prefatory Remarks" to the Dora case (see Chapters 1 and 5 of this book), I am inclined to doubt the full reliability of Freud's report of material concerning the second dream. We are given to believe that on December 31, 1900, Dora recalled that the trauma had happened *exactly* two and a half years previously (June 30, 1898) and that exactly two weeks afterward (*July* 14) she had told her parents about the incident. Supposedly, then, Freud had to explain to her that her two weeks of waiting was the same amount of time a governess about to quit would give.

In conveying the sequel to the lakeside events, Freud gives us this exchange.

"A few days after I had left he sent me a picture post-card."
"Yes, but when after that nothing more came, you gave free rein to your feelings of revenge. I can even imagine that at that time you were still able to find room for a subsidiary intention, and thought that your accusation might be a means of inducing

23. For another criticism of Freud's interpretation, see Sand, 1983, 352–353.

him to travel to the place where you were living." . . . "As he actually offered to do at first," Dora threw in. . . . "In that way your longing for him would have been appeased"—here she nodded assent, a thing which I had not expected. (107)

Dora's bare verbal reply is suggestive, yet we again question whether Freud vitiated it editorially. Or did he minimize the impact of Hans's lying about, vilification of, and continued victimization of Dora? Freud strategically attempts to have the reader deny the ambiguity of Dora's nod and interpret it as univocal assent. We might wonder, in opposition to Freud, whether that gesture might have been a sign of silent recognition that Dora knew where Freud was heading, although she disagreed with him.

But rather than dwell on that debatable point, let us return to Freud's next, long interpretation to Dora. In midflight Freud expatiates: "It is true that two years ago you were very young. But you told me yourself that your mother was engaged at seventeen and then waited two years for her husband. A daughter usually takes her mother's love-story as her model. So you too wanted to wait for him, and you took it that he was only waiting till you were grown up enough to be his wife" (108). After elaborating, Freud once more implies that Dora agreed: "Dora had listened to me without any of her usual contradictions. She seemed to be moved; she said goodbye to me very warmly" (108–109). But again, we object, how could she have agreed? Had she voiced the facts, her disagreement would have demonstrated how he grossly had misread her silence. Whereas Käthe was in fact engaged at the age of seventeen, Dora was but fifteen and a half at the lakeside incident. Because Dora could not have taken her mother as model in the chronological way Freud assumed, we may conclude that she was too fed up with Freud to correct his patent chronological error. He was tightly leashed to his story, and she left him there.

Surprised that Dora's decision to quit came "so unexpectedly" (109), Freud forgot that he had already detected that decision in her first dream. And what justification did Freud have for saying that the treatment ended when his "hopes of a successful termination . . . were at their highest" (109)? Dora told him of her decision to "put up with" (105) the therapy until the end of the year, indicating that she had had enough of Freud. In the incendiary finality of the last session, Freud resembled Käthe, who, in her single-minded concern for her jewels, was oblivious of those imperiled around her. And when he declared, "You are free to stop the treatment at any time. But for today we will go on with our work" (105), he resembled Hans: such a declaration is surely more appropriately addressed to a maid than to a patient.[24]

Instead of examining the immediate issue of termination, Freud demonstrated Dora's second-rate personal importance to him by dealing with his own agenda of dream interpretation and genetic reconstruction until the very end. He found complex meanings in Dora's second dream—revenge; tender heterosexual and homosexual feelings; positive and negative fantasies of being deflowered, pregnant, and waiting for requited love—but he simplified her termination of treatment, calling it "an unmistakable act of vengeance on her part" (109). And although he believed that Dora's refusal of Hans hid her desire for him to repeat his advances and thereby confirm his love, Freud did not consider the possibility of such contradictory meanings in her decision to terminate. He also overlooked other possibilities which might have been felt most intensely at this extreme moment: her desire to flee Freud's burning office, from which she would not be secure until she truly woke up outside; her desire to stay and seduce; her desire to stay and be seduced.

Since Freud had promised Dora a cure in a year, why did he not interpret Dora's quitting after nearly three months of therapy —during the season of Christmas and New Year, which could foster conception fantasies—as her symbolic way of avoiding being impregnated by him? Her remaining time amounted to approximately nine months, after all. Clearly Freud's aim was not that Dora stay and resolve the transference but rather that he obtain "conclusive proof" of her love for Hans and discover her

24. See Glenn's cogent article (1986).

self-reproach behind her father's disbelief of the lake scene (46, 59). A later comment by Freud glosses the whole, particularly the end of his treatment of Dora: "Regretfully, only a few patients are worth the trouble we spend on them, so that *we are not allowed to have a therapeutic attitude, but we must be glad to have learned something in every case*" (my italics).[25]

Freud's countertransferential bitterness toward Dora made him fail as a follow-up therapist when she came back two years later to deal with a facial neuralgia. Although this time she came with a request for treatment that was her own, he refused to see her afterward and linked her facial neuralgia with a newspaper report that she had read two weeks previously about his professorial appointment. With omniscient self-justification, he proclaims that one glance at her face sufficed to prove her insincerity in wanting further treatment. But whose insincerity is at stake? The grudging tone throughout the case history belies his statement that he promised "to forgive" her for depriving him of the satisfaction of bringing her a "far more radical" release from her sufferings (122). Did Freud's rejection of Dora in 1902 help drive her into marriage the following year?

On the positive side, it is safe to say that for Dora learning about her repressed love for her father and Hans dissipated her suicidal ideation and to a certain degree some of her more intense depressive complaints. Freud did succeed in being the first to hear of the shop kiss; he did believe her about the scene and the parental collusion, thus validating some of her sense of reality, so long frustrated. Months after her treatment ended, she confronted the Zellenkas about their collusion. Yet once more adopting an anti-overdeterministic stance, Freud considered Dora's search to verify the truth as vengeful, not healthy; for him it was either-or, not both-and. The importance of validation was so crucial for Dora that only after persuading the Zellenkas to rescind their denial did she proceed to seek out Freud. When Dora told Freud

25. Freud's letter of June 11, 1922, to Weiss (Weiss, 1970, 37).

about validating her experience with Zellenkas, was it also to have herself revalidated? Was it to have her desire to recontinue treatment validated?

From Dora's dream texts in this chapter we pass on to Freud's textuality, which bears subtle traces of his own oneiric life. He dreamt and he wrote more than he meant, and he did not stop trying to mean.

5

Psychodynamics in Freud's Textuality

It's the subtlest thing I have written so far.

There remains much to understand about the gendered ramifications of Freud's personal life. Gender shaded his view of the chief polarities in our mental life: passivity and activity, the ego and the external world, pleasure and unpleasure. In particular, he equated the passive with the feminine, the weak, and the morally negative, and he unconsciously extended this equation into his unconscious conceptions of the oedipal complex, narcissism, masochism, and even religion.[1]

Gender also played a salient role in Freud's thinking about historical figures. He identified with a long line of them, all male, in the political, cultural, scientific, artistic, and religious spheres. He also entertained eroticized conceptions of the cultural world powers: France, England, Greece, Rome, Egypt. In his symbolic geography he thus established a gendered linkage between England and masculinity, on the one hand, and France and femininity, on the other. That polarity collapsed in the ambiguous symbiosis characterizing his encounter with Rome. From that dynamic, Freud proceeded to journey in two directions: he pictured the Moses of Michelangelo as a model of masculine moral control; and, in the opening decades of the twentieth century, he conceived of Egypt as the land of primal motherhood and bisexuality. But the

1. On femininity and passivity, see Schafer (1977), but the definitive commentary is by Davis (1993).

Egypt imagined by the later Freud is very different. Ignoring his previous linkage of Egypt with bisexuality, he now saw it as a culture—instanced in the person of Moses—marked by masculine cultural achievements. In sum, a dualism worked itself out again and again in Freud's explorations of culture. In the 1880s, to his way of thinking, puritan, manly England was in opposition to fascinating, feminine Paris; in the 1890s anxiogenic Rome, with its threat of masculine papal power, merged with the church as Holy Mother; in the 1910s virile Michelangelo sharply differed from androgynous Leonardo; and finally, culminating in Freud's "Moses and Monotheism," Egypt, the land of primal bisexual culture, was confronted with the enlightened patriarchal despotism of Moses (Schorske, 1993).[2]

The powerful mother, it should be said, was never absent from Freud's symbolic geography. Early on, the United States, the transatlantic embodiment of the feminized dark continent, was powerful and hateful to him. A gendered geographic-historical split permitted him to revise his history of humankind; he identified with the exiled masculine Moses and, as I have shown (1993, 1995), depreciated his own mother-goddess, subjecting her to banishment across the ocean.

More immediate to his professional concerns was an overriding goal in all of Freud's work: to plumb the secrets of nature, which for him was a maternal object. The memorable published essay "Nature," which Freud heard in a public reading and which influenced him to switch from philosophy to medicine, contains these eroticized identifications of Nature: "She dwells in none but children; and the mother, where is she?—She is the sole artist: from the simplest stuff to the greatest contrasts; without apparent effort, to the greatest perfection . . . [s]he enacts a drama. . . . There is an eternal life, a coming into being, and a movement in her. . . . She loves herself and through eyes and hearts without number she clings to herself. She has analyzed herself in order to enjoy

---

2. In his fascinating article Schorske also details Freud's overdetermined conceptions of the historical capitals of cultural power.

herself. . . . She has set me within. She will also lead me without. I commit myself to her."[3]

Gendered identification overshadowed Freud's own investigations. In many ways, his ego-ideal as an investigator was Leonardo da Vinci, whom he held to be the first modern man and the first since the Greeks to rely only on his observation and judgment in exploring the secrets of nature. Freud's praise of the anti-authoritarian da Vinci sounds autobiographical: "If we translate scientific abstraction back again into concrete individual experience, we see that the 'ancients' and authority simply correspond to his father, and nature once more becomes the tender and kindly mother who had nourished him" (1910, 122). Freud's comments on da Vinci to the Vienna Psychoanalytic Society followed in the same vein: "But this absence of prejudice too is determined by his relationship to his parents: all along to be himself from old age [i.e., father] and to return to Mother[!] Nature—principles that he repeatedly advocated in public" (Nunberg and Federn, 1967, 348; the brackets are the editors'). Yet if Nature, the object of Freud's study, was feminine, his very investigative means—analytic penetration—was linked with the masculine. And Freud communicated that penetration in a textuality that he also gendered.

Let us note that the scriptive transmission of psychoanalysis was charged for Freud and extended even to his correspondence. He invested in the mechanics and scenic elements of writing: handwriting (reflecting on one of his letters he later mentioned how his handwriting had changed four times—Freud, 1965, 268); the use and spacing of Gothic letters in German, which facilitated his inspiration; the quality and size of his stationery and its heading; the kinds of pens that he employed and the colors of ink; the length of any letter; and the overall timing of his response. In a letter to Ferenczi, Freud (1993b, 138) even drew attention to the psychological implications of how he himself

3. The essay, which Freud mistakenly believed to have been written by Goethe, is conveniently reprinted in Wittels, 1931, 31ff.

folded the writing paper (Freud, 1994, 138).[4] Freud also graphically described that coitus may be symbolized by "writing, which
entails making a liquid flow out of a tube onto a piece of white
paper" (1926, 90). He could even animate a text: its "distortions
resemble a murder" (1939, 43). But my main point is that Freud
not only personified a text but gendered it—particularly in his
case histories, in which writing is a sexually symbolic map of
Freud's and his patients' bodies.

For specific examples of the symbolic geography found in
Freud's texts, let us begin with *The Interpretation of Dreams,* Freud's
own case history. In the Dreambook he sets his epistemological
investigation in a narrative framework of travel through nature.
Insofar as nature symbolized the female body for Freud, he married his scientific exposition to an oedipal and then preoedipal
journey through the maternal corpus. Recapitulating the overall
procedure of his self-analysis, the dream about self-dissection
concerns two books: the first, Rider Haggard's novel *She,* which
Freud summed up as "full of hidden meaning, the eternal feminine" (1900, 453); and the second, the ongoing and highly symbolic *Interpretation of Dreams* itself, which occasioned his dreaming
about dissection.[5]

Freud's gendered textuality also characterizes the cases of the
Rat Man and the Wolf Man. The Rat Man himself felt his utterances to be an extension of his own feminized corporeal schema.
He resorted to abbreviation and rapid pronunciation to prevent
words from "inserting" or "creeping" like imagined rats between
the members of his speech. On the other hand, and so true to his
ambivalence, he spoke indistinctly, thus provoking his listener to
ask that the obscure articulation be repeated, slowed down, and

4. In a beautiful study Mijolla (1989) shows that Freud established a veritable
graphic ritual.
5. In Freud's words: "The dissection meant the self-analysis which I *am*
carrying out, as it were, in the publication of this present book about dreams"
(1900, 481/477; the italics show where I correct the distorting use of the past tense
in *S.E.*). Freud's dissection and writing combine as simultaneous performative acts
to create and dissect a corpus that is the written material itself.

spaced. By the same token, the Rat Man as listener was wont to have his interlocutors repeat themselves and introduce notable spaces into their utterances. Everywhere the Rat Man disrupted contiguity, created gaps and symbolic anuses to be penetrated, or phobically closed up such gaps.

When we turn from the Rat Man as patient to Freud's exposition of the case, we come upon a surprise: the evidence of contiguity disturbance, present in the Rat Man's phobic attitude to touching, continued into the textuality of Freud's case history. Atypically his writing in the case is shot through with disconnectedness—to such an extent that we must suspect countertransferential interference. Indeed, Freud's written expression in this case history is infected by its subject matter, obsessional neurosis, a pathology that can influence both the awareness and the expression of contiguous relationships. Instead of encountering the familiar Freud with his superb articulateness, we come upon a bungling writer who confuses the precipitating causes of the Rat Man's adult disorder; who elaborates but little on the links among the heterosexual object choices in his patient's adult life; who does not enmesh clinical and theoretical considerations as firmly as he does elsewhere; who does not neat tie together child and adult symptomatology; and who does not integrate main explanatory perspectives, such as economic theory, ambivalence, and anality.

Significantly, when Freud first delivered the case history of the Rat Man in the form of a lecture, he called it a "potpourri of particular observations and general remarks" (1974, 141). Even more significantly, when Freud later started to write up the case, he again was aware of its disconnectedness, for, as we know from two letters to Jung, he considered qualifying it by introducing the word "aphorisms" into the general title (1974, 145, 159). And what are aphorisms? Well, they are concise general statements that are isolated from one another; usually there are no verbal ligatures between them. Notably, in Freud's introduction to this case history, he repeatedly refers to its disconnectedness (the repetitions are obscured in the *Standard Edition*).

Although the most dramatic evidence of anal eroticism appears in many pages of the first, clinical part of the Rat Man case, anality is mentioned only once, and in a footnote at that, in the second, theoretical section. But nowhere does Freud recognize anal-sadistic regression as essential to obsessional neurosis; nowhere does he trace the causal connection between anal eroticism and obsessional neurosis. Instead, Freud—seemingly inhibited by the very pathology he is explaining—"isolates" anality and thereby disrupts its intrinsic connection with obsessional neurosis ("isolation," we remember, refers to the use of temporal intervals in order to disrupt "causal connections"—1909, 246).

All in all, the case history, a report of symptomatic speaking, listening, and interpreting all enmeshed, is in itself a symptomatic writing. In none of his other writings did Freud complain so helplessly about an aphoristic style that disrupts linkage among units of discourse of various lengths. That disruption or disconnectedness, I offer, might be related to the fact that Freud had not yet discovered the essence of obsessional neurosis to be a regression from oedipal conflict to anal eroticism. I postulate further that although Freud formally assigned an energetically defined thinking process to be the organizing factor in obsessional neurosis, he unconsciously perceived the centrality of an anal eroticism that, as a return of the repressed, made its scriptive appearance as voids, gaps, disconnectedness between groups of statements. Like the gaps in dream reports, these can symbolize the female genitalia and also the castration of the male dreamer. Those compositional traces of feminization cut deep in Freud's text, symbolically his own corpus (Mahony, 1986a).

If, as I have discussed (1994), the textuality of *The Interpretation of Dreams* symbolically represented the maternal body that Freud unconsciously investigated with his own preoedipal and oedipal strivings, the textuality of "From the History of an Infantile Neurosis" (1918) reflexively inscribed Freud's struggle with a castrated corporeal schema and its supposed restoration. Beyond the interactions between Freud and the Wolf Man and their textual description, the dynamic of castration, I would also propose, left its impress on the partial reading of the case by idealizing and self-castrating readers.

In exploring the Wolf Man's primal scene, Freud maps three points of orientation: the prototype, the subsequent substitutes for the prototype, and the lacunae found in the sequence of the substitutes. Attention to the quest of this triad prepares us to detect that the Wolf Man's personal and clinical history and Freud's text of that history are marked by feminine identification and castration. Preoccupied by the etiological quest to find the head of the Nile (1896a, 203), Freud constantly strove to identify *Vorbild,* or the prototype of psychic phenomena. He crisscrossed the case of the Wolf Man with references to the *Vorbild,* as either objects or events; for example, the Wolf Man's hostility toward God found its prototype in hostility toward his father, and the child's defecation was the prototype of castration. As he pursued the prototypes in his patient's life, Freud came upon an impressive array of multiple substitute objects and events, ranging from wolves, to childhood teachers, to masturbation.

Freud states that within the sequences of prototype and substitute abound gaps (*Lücke*), incompleteness (*Unvollständigkeit*), and something that is missing (*fehlen*), which he tries over and over to fill (*erfüllen, ausfüllen*). Anxious to thwart the castrating derivatives[6] in the patient's story from spilling over into the textuality of the case history and subverting it, Freud was ready to find or to reconstruct fill-ins that would simultaneously complete the evolutionary picture of the Wolf Man's feminization and ward off the invagination of Freud's textuality.

There is one explanatory condition, Freud continues, that the Wolf Man's determining nightmare had to "fulfill" (*erfüllen*): it had "to create a conviction [*Überzeugung*] of the reality of the

---

6. For Freud, all the texts of symptoms, dreams, associations, and transference are to be "translated" (*übersetzen;* cf. *S.E.,* "explained") or submitted to the "arts of translation" by the analyst (*Übersetzungskünste,* 280/116; cf. *S.E.,* "explanatory arts"). For other comments on the term "translation" as well as the more general subject of translating Freud, see Ornston (1992); Ornston's anthology excels not only in the essays included but also for its bibliography.

existence of castration" (Freud, 1918, 36). The German root of *überzeugen* is *zeugen*, which means both "to witness" and "to procreate"—thus the two actions of the primal scene, that of the perceiving child and that of the copulating parents. Freud was keenly aware of that lexical complexity of *Überzeugung*, as is evident in the Rat Man case (1909, 233n) and in comments to the Vienna Psychoanalytic Society in 1910, the same year that he began to analyze the Wolf Man (Nunberg and Federn, 1974, 63). The first five chapters of the Wolf Man case are focused on the primal scene. And it is quite to the point that nowhere else in the entire Freudian corpus have I detected so frequent a usage of *überzeugen*—some twenty times, or one per three pages. The manifest meaning of the overdetermined verb points to Freud's persuasive aims with both his patient and his readership; its latent meaning embraces the primal scene. If *überzeugen* were spelled out in a proposition, we could hear the persons involved quickly alternate as grammatical subject and object; but as the matter stands, the primal scene is subtly condensed within the letter of Freud's rhetorical strategy.

In the Wolf Man case Freud explained *Nachträglichkeit* (deferred effect) in terms of its dual temporal directionality, prospective as well as retrospective. Such duality reappears as an expository device reflected in the constant textual anticipations and retrogressive or recapitulating movements in Freud's case history. Though a hallmark of Freud's style at large, this expository device—or scanning technique, as I have elsewhere named it (1987a)—recurs very often in the Wolf Man case, especially in chapter 4, the case's showpiece, where Freud introduces the wolf dream. I propose that the textual bidirectionality in this chapter, its self-reflexive prospective and retrospective repetition, is mimetic of the spatial bidirectionality or backward and forward movement of the coitus a tergo embedded within the wolf dream.

The coital and witnessing activities of the primal scene and Freud's persuasive aim regarding those activities are condensed in *überzeugen*. That nodal point, referring to the primal scene in general, is complemented by another nodal point, *Nachträglichkeit*, which refers to the positional distinctiveness of the Wolf

Man's primal scene, *more ferarum*. The forward and backward movements of coition from behind find a descriptive partner both in the self-reflexive backward and forward movements, the shuttling, of Freud's prose and in the retrospective and forward-looking meanings of *Nachträglichkeit*. Freud's fantasy of feminization and castration, therefore, fosters his discursive urge to fill in textual gaps, to embed charged meanings in nodal words, and to fashion a coituslike movement in his prose (Mahony, 1995). Now let us examine the Dora case as text. Freud's title for the Dora case, "Fragment of an Analysis of a Case of Hysteria," sounds drily descriptive, like those of his other case histories: "Analysis of a Phobia in a Five-Year-Old Boy," "Notes upon a Case of Obsessional Neurosis," "Psychoanalytic Notes on an Autobiographical Account of a Case of Paranoia (Dementia Paranoides)," and "From the History of an Infantile Neurosis." Why Freud avoided poetic or suggestive titles, like those of his other writings, is not certain, although we may guess that he wanted to contain the fictivity and contagious fantasy amply present in his case histories.

The truism that psychoanalysis is like a second chance at correcting adolescent development has an analogy in the fact that Freud's case history of Dora modified his understanding of her treatment. Freud overlooked much that was crucial until the end or after the end of the case, with the result that its write-up is a writing-through and a writing-out or, to say it neologistically, a writing-through-out. Indeed, we can apply Freud's comment on transference and symptoms to his own countertransference: the symptoms "disappear a little while later, when the relations between patient and physician have been dissolved" (115). Far from dissolving his countertransference toward Dora, Freud enacted it with the reader, whom he also tried to pressure and seduce into complicitous agreement.

During the treatment Freud dealt with Dora's oedipal conflicts as he understood them at the time, but his write-up represents a kind of secondary revision.[7] To be more exact, his writing-

---

7. The relation between Freud's textual metaphor and the translation of his texts deserves clarification. For him, transferences are new editions or facsimiles of

up of the case history bears its own preoedipal and oedipal meanings, which overlap or modify the polysemy of the treatment. If Dora refused to submit to the exchange required by Freud's marriage plan, he, by publishing the case, could put her into circulation, this time the way he wanted. Serving as a follow-up to Dora's treatment, Freud's composition is a well-orchestrated condemnation of her.

In his "Prefatory Remarks," Freud does not explicitly mention Dora at all, except for the terminal footnote added in 1923. In chapter 1, "The Clinical Picture," Freud introduces Dora (15–18), then reports Philip's story (18–27), creating a double male containment of Dora. Only from page 27 on does Freud let Dora tell her own story, but not completely, for he interlards it with his own reconstruction (up to page 32). So who spoke for Dora, who lost her voice? In Freud's repeated textual blurring of what material consonant with his position came from her rather than from himself, he assimilated her into a textual marriage that he mastered alone. The unfolding of Freud's narrative can be seen another way. He depicts his hostile medical colleagues as his main enemy, then has Dora join ranks with them, only to become the chief target of his attack. Meanwhile, he maneuvers his sympathetic readers onto center stage, addressing them directly and behind Dora's back.

More than a simple script of the therapeutic drama and more than deferred effect, Freud's scriptive follow-up instantiates its own misunderstanding and understanding. It is in the "Postscript" that Freud discloses that the transference is a psychic postscript, a revised edition. When he avows not having mastered transference during the treatment, he is truly saying, wittingly or not, that his written text is the emergent trace of the revised text, that is, the transference belatedly recognized. Better yet, as a secondary elab-

-----

fantasies and impulses activated by the analysis. Claiming to keep his metaphor, he then makes a distinction between transferences that are merely reprints, and others, more "artfully" (*kunstvoller*) constructed, that are revised editions. Adhering to Freud's own metaphor, we may conclude that his writing of the case history is a revision of a revised edition.

oration, the write-up is a revision of the transferential revision. In line with the conception of transference as text, countertransference constitutes another textual episode in Freud's life story. The sexualization of the therapy and its aggressive, penetrating interpretations carry over into the eroticization of its write-up. He symbolically scripts his body into both the content and the form of the case history; and his own symptomatology, interacting with that of Dora and of her significant objects, is inscribed in the writing. Reminiscent of the sexually "symbolic geography" (99) of Dora's dream and dictated to considerable extent by his unconscious as ghost writer, Freud's symptomatic writing incorporates traces of damaged body schema.

If Freud figures forth unconscious aspects of transference in complementary scriptive and printing terms, such as revisions and new editions, he also projects his unconscious fantasy about the body onto the complementary content and form of his textuality. Certain formal aspects of his textuality—noncompletion, fragmentation, gaps—eminently represent Freud himself, who was castrated by Dora's resistance, which culminated in abrupt termination. His inscriptive enactment, a meaningful performance in its own right, dramatizes the fragile claims of patriarchal sexuality.

For Freud, a diagnostic indication of strictly organic pathology is that the patient may produce a perfectly clear and connected narration 16–17n). By contrast—and Freud could not have stated it more clearly—a hysteric's self-narrative is perforce undercut by loss or failure of memory, a deficiency that points to hysterical symptoms. Although Freud realizes that his case history is not nicely rounded off, he steers clear of linking any failure of his textuality with his own conflicts. His alleged greater concern is the narrative of the other, which he describes with marvelous insight: "The patients' inability to give an ordered history of their life insofar as it coincides with the history of their illness is not merely characteristic of the neurosis. It also possesses great theoretical significance. . . . [The faultiness of] memories relating to the history of the illness is *a necessary correlate of the symptoms and one which is theoretically requisite* (16–18)." Thus Freud castigates medical doctors for their "smooth and precise" histories—in fact, they are surreptitious artists. In contrast, Freud announces himself as the true doctor and wants his readers to share in that medical assessment: *"If I were to begin* by giving a full and consistent case history, it would place the reader in a very different situation from that of the medical observer" (16, my italics). More often than not, he opts for the inductive method, thereby having us join him in observing the development of the case.

Yet Freud's confusion about the chronological order of events, when explained by his own theory, puts him in the category of hysterical patients who cannot give a reliable narrative. Grappling with Dora's transferential and homosexual material makes him like one of his hysterical patients who cannot tell a coherent self-narrative. In a manner revelatory of his own conflicts, he does not textually interrelate the themes of transference and homosexuality as he did the supposed dissolution of transference and symptoms. As readers of the case, we are familiar with the quasi absence of transference during Dora's therapy and its textual prominence in the "Postscript." We recall, too, the peculiar presence of homosexual references as afterthoughts in the last paragraph in section 1, in the awkwardly long, belated, and terminal footnotes in section 3 (105–106, 110–111), and in a footnote in the "Postscript" (120). Hence, although the themes of transference and homosexuality figure in the "Postscript," they remain typographically separate from each other, a sign of their nonintegration. Freud consigns the underlying homosexuality to the literal subtext of a footnote. Freud the analyst, scientific researcher, and expositor felt overcome, even castrated, by four forces: his wound from wrestling with such unconscious matter as homosexuality; Dora's curtailment of the case, which frustrated his penetrating male interpretations; the inability of his "arts of translation" (*Übersetzungskünste,* 280/116) to alter his patient's symptoms, which were reinforced by secondary gain; and the incapacity of textuality per se to convey both the process and the results of the treatment. In an unwilling aping of Dora, who abruptly broke off her treatment, Freud himself effected a "shortening" (*Verkürzung*) of his report, for he felt unable both to simultaneously communicate analytic results and "to complete the other task" (*die andere Aufgabe zu erfüllen*) of depicting the analytic process (170/13).

To appreciate the nuances of Freud's bleak reportorial and clinical picture, we should be aware that he uses the term "to solve" (*lösen*) ambiguously to mean "to figure out, to resolve, such as a riddle," 31, 32n, 46), or "to dissolve (such as a symptom)."[8] Symptoms disappear but not right away, for only after treatment is ended is the transference "dissolved" (*gelöst*, 279/115), and only after that transference has been "resolved" (*Lösung*, 280/117) does the patient believe the constructions heard in psychoanalysis. In Freud's opinion, his treatment of Dora could do no more than "manage" (*Erledigung leisten*) the case.[9] If, however, a treatment is carried to its appropriate end, the patient's narrative—previously marked by gaps and with inaccurate information filling some of those gaps—becomes "intelligible, consistent, and unbroken" (*lückenlose*, 175/18). Yet that restoration is precisely what Dora undercut.

8. In the Dora case and elsewhere, Strachey sometimes translates *Lösung* (solution) and *lösen* (to solve) with "resolve" (280/117) or "dissolve" (279/115).
9. Strachey softens this ambiguous term, rendering it as "effected . . . relief" (171n/14n; in the passages about the second dream, Strachey more properly translates *Erledigung* as "had been dealt with," 256/94). Critics relying wholly on *S.E.* are prone to error. For instance, Gallop (1982, 142) draws our attention to the end of Dora case as found in *S.E.* (109): "It must be confessed that Dora's father was not entirely straightforward." In Gallop's view, " 'It must be confessed' suggests that some shame attached to this for Freud. He has been taken in, believing in this man's 'interest' and 'support, and then discovering he was merely being used." In fact, however, the German equivalent for "It must be confessed" is not to be found in the *Gesammelte Werke*; the phrase is Strachey's elegant addition to the translated passage. This circumstance is just one more indication that in using the English *Concordance* to Freud's works, researchers must proceed with the utmost caution. The *Concordance* is accurate for Strachey, but not for Freud. Another example is Strachey's translation of the note added by Freud to the Dora case history in 1923 (13–14n). Freud writes that he declines to bring the case "up to date" and then adds, "*sie dem heutigen Stande unseres Wissen anzupassen*" (and to fit it in with the present state of our knowledge). Strachey did not translate this last statement.

The overdetermined and quasi-compulsive references to incompleteness—"broken off," "fragment," "gap," "complete," and "incomplete"—recur as textual indicators of a castration conflict. Matching the labeling of the case as fragmentary and incomplete, Freud explicitly describes his incomplete analytic results as "mutilated relics" (*verstümmelten Reste*, 169/12). The very first word of the German title for the case, *Bruchstück*, is not just a fragment; literally, it is a broken piece," a double fragment. Significantly, Freud changed the original title of the published case ("Dreams and Hysteria") to stress not its content but its nature as a fragment. Freud also "breaks off" (*unterbreche*) his discussion of clinical material to treat dream theory (229/67). In his "Postscript" specifically, Freud calls attention to his case history as a fragment and adds that the case is even more fragmentary than the titular word indicates (112).[10] Again and again in chapter 1 Freud admits not being able to complete the treatment and the analysis of the dream, that is, not being able to "complement" (*ergänzen*) and penetrate either Dora or her feminized symbol, the dream—he fails with the woman twice over. In fact, so shaken was Freud by the aborted treatment that in every major section of his case history he specifies that the case was "broken off" by the patient (12, 13n, 112).[11]

To follow what gaps precisely meant for Freud, we may return to *The Interpretation of Dreams*, which he mentioned over half a dozen times in the Dora case history. In the Dreambook we read that the form or structure of a dream may have a symbolic meaning. The gaps or missing parts in the dream of a male patient, Freud insists, bear a sexual symbolism: "The 'gaps' [*Lücken*] were

---

10. Like some familiar untrustworthy narrator in modernist fiction, Freud pauses at regular intervals to remind readers of the case history that "my insight into the complex of events composing it has remained fragmentary" (see Marcus, 1976, 405–406). Elsewhere Marcus astutely remarks that in part Freud wrote the Dora case history as a way of "dealing with, mastering, expressing, and neutralizing" material that troubled him (440); "he had to write it out, in some measure, as an effort of self-understanding" (408).

11. My elaboration partly concurs with Moi's perceptive, highly condensed insights (1981); see especially 16–18.

the genital apertures of the women who were going to bed; and 'there's something missing' described the principal feature of the female genitalia" (1900, 333; *G.W.*, 2/3:338).

If "a dream stands, as it were, upon two legs" (71), if the dream is the genitalia, then Freud's own dreamlike text is concerned with the state of its symbolic genitalia. Pertinently enough, the theme of gaps recurs in theoretical and clinical passages in the case history; Breuer's hypnoid theory, for example, introduces a gap, or "breaks off" (*unterbrechen*) the continuity, between trauma and symptom formation (185n/27n). The evidence for Dora's masturbation is without gap (241/78), but the story about why and when Dora forsook the practice is full of gaps (242/79). Freud himself tries to overcome any gap in dating the recurrences of Dora's lakeside dream (66)

Truly, Freud presents us with an erotics of narrative enactment. As a compromise formation, his text is a conscious explanation as well as unconscious enactment of his theory. In other words, his text is not just about psychosexuality; it is a textualized psychosexuality. Let us see how Freud's text performs its theme of castration.

From the "Prefatory Remarks":

The treatment was . . . broken off.

The treatment . . . was broken off.

From chapter 1:

The following fragment . . . [is not] a full [*lückenlose*, "gapless"] and consistent case history.

In the further course of the treatment . . . the gaps [*Lücken*] in memory are filled in. It is only towards the end of the treatment that we have before us an intelligible, consistent, and unbroken [*lückenlose*] case history.

[[T]he treatment of the case, and consequently my insight . . . remain fragmentary . . . reconstruction . . . a supplement [*Ergänzung*, literally, "completion," 189/31].

[T]here were *"no gaps"* [*keine Lücke*, 190/32] in Dora's memory concerning the interaction between her father and Mrs. K.

From chapter 2:

The circumstantial evidence of her having masturbated in childhood seems to be complete and without a flaw [*lückenlos*, literally, "without gaps"].

[O]wing to the incompleteness of the analysis I present fragmentary material [*lückenhaftes*, literally, "with many gaps"].

Unfortunately, an incomplete analysis cannot enable us to follow the chronological sequence of the changes in a symptom's meaning.

It is only because the analysis was prematurely broken off that we have been obliged in Dora's case to resort to framing conjectures.

Whatever I have brought forward for filling up the gaps [*Ausfüllung der Lücken*] is based upon other cases which have been more thoroughly analyzed.

I unfortunately left a gap [*Lücke*] in the analysis of the dream.

From chapter 3:

[T]he analysis was broken off.

[The dream] filled a gap in her memory.

[I]f the analysis had been continued . . .

Her breaking off so unexpectedly . . . was an unmistakable act of vengeance on her part.

From chapter 4:

I have introduced this paper as a fragment of an analysis; but the reader will have discovered that it is incomplete to a far greater degree than its title might have led him to expect.

. . . work was broken off.

I have published a fragment in these pages.

[The case] was broken off prematurely.

[She demonstrated my] helplessness and incapacity [in her] fragmentary treatment.

Clearly, Freud felt deeply that both his treatment and his text were massively mutilated. Reflective of that mutilation (and perhaps also of Freud's unconscious desire to deflower Dora?), the verb "to tear" (*reissen*) shows up in a surprising variety of contexts. Freud admits that he had no hope of "removing" (*entreissen*, 163/7) the objections of his critics. In dreams, numbers are often "torn" (*gerissen*, 259n/97) out of their true context. In the memory, a connection between events can be "torn apart" (*zerrissen*, 175/17; see also 174/16). Dora "tore herself away" from Hans (*riss sich los*, 186/28). Previously she had prevented doctors from "tearing away" (*entreissen*, 241, 78) her secret, whereas now she was hinting that she would soon allow her secret to be torn away away from her. In the very last sentence of the case we read about her wanting to "tear herself free" from her father (*losreissen*, 286/122).

In responding to castration, Freud resorted to measures of symbolic self-restoration during the treatment, a contrast to the combined self-restoration and self-vindication in the write-up. Because he was unable to fully penetrate Dora's mystery, he reacted by composing a scriptive compromise formation, a symbolic geography of a projected body schema. His result not fully succeeding, Freud now had to shrug off the dual castration of his text and his treatment. Reaching into his cornucopia of sour grapes, he whines that the truncation of the case is closely linked with its "unusual clarity" (118); that a complete text would be nearly unreadable (112); and that anyhow, as things stand, he expects to be criticized for textual excess, for giving uncalled-for information about Dora. To the extent that his write-up is also incoherent, we may qualify it as a symptomatic reaction and pseudo-restoration. However hard he endeavored at critical points to repair the patient's memory and replace her symptoms with his own symptomatic fantasies and reconstructions, he could not lock her up completely in his textual closet.[12]

Lexical references to self-restoration, "completion" (*Ergänzung*), and "fulfillment" (*Erfüllung*) abound in Freud's text. The keynote is located in the very first sentence of chapter 1 of the Dora case: *The Interpretation of Dreams* shows that dream interpretation serves as a means of "filling in" amnesias (reconstruction was another means; for instance, Dora's story was "completed" by an erection, 247/84). In his role as a writer Freud also feels forced to overcome other gaps with completions (247/85, 201/42) and admits to having "restored what is missing" (*das Unvollständige . . . ergänzt,* 169/12). Yet he does not always abide by his promise that at every point he will show where the raw clinical material ends and his reconstructions begin (12).[13]

Self-restoration was a more subtle matter, for the symptomatic nature of Freud's textual fill-ins made it an unfulfilled wish. During the therapy Freud kept Dora's paternal and seductive transferences at bay, and he overlooked completely the female transference; urged on by an intensified masculine identification during the writing of the case, Freud tried to repair his castrated male parts and further repress his female identification. If in the assaultive interpretations of his fragmentary text, Freud resembles Hans, he also fights not to be like the impotent Philip. We might see Freud expressing his triumphant self-vindication in the male genderlect of the time: "Despite Dora, I got something out of her."

In the end, we must say that Freud's filled-in fragment is

12. From another point of view, Marcus (1976, 405) perceptively comments that Freud's case is "simultaneously fragmentary and complete. Thus, like a modernist writer—which in part he is—Freud begins by elaborately announcing the problematic status of his undertaking and the dubious character of his achievement. . . . [Freud's] method is hence a fragmentary construction and reconstruction which in the end amount to a whole that simultaneously retains its disjointed character—in sum it resembles 'reality' itself." For another study of the resemblance between Freud's case and modernist literature, see van den Berg, 1987. For other fine comments on Freud's narrative, see also Sprengnether, 1985; Bernheimer, 1985; Kahane, 1985; Sulieman, 1988; and Roof, 1991.

13. Reinforcing his scriptive attempt at self-recuperation, Freud visited the highly symbolic Rome not many weeks afterward (Glenn, 1986).

more satisfying than many a "complete" psychiatric case. So Freud's case is complete and not complete, a corpus dually symbolizing his castration and his overdetermined and vengeful self-restoration. And Dora was more than Dora. She stood, too, for an enigmatic configuration of woman and for an enigmatic configuration of Fliess, a circumstance rousing Freud to write another dream-text, which itself had begun in his long-buried infantile past and which—like a somatic disorder that for decades can accumulate symptomatic meanings from any source—intruded into the rich reserve of nightlight, Dora's dreams. After a lifetime waiting to be delivered, Freud's dream-text bursts forth with a shifting array of discursive modes and cognitive views: description, narration, dramatization, argumentation, demonstration, uncontained dissemination of figurative language, dazzling reasoning, assured understanding, irony, skepticism, and rash presumption.[14] A psychic desolation pervades the whole. There is no instance of mature conviviality, gratitude, joy, laughter, altruism, or gentleness. And intensifying that psychic desolation is a stark natural landscape and total or nigh-total absence of beauty, color, harmonious sound, gratifying taste, and fragrance. In short, the scene is finely wrought but rather chilling.

Although we have already seen how both Freud and Dora were prisoners of their defective interwoven narratives, an area deserving of elaboration is their involvement with reproachfulness. Freud resembles Dora both as clinician and as case writer. From the very beginning of his case, Freud strikes a note of reproach. He defends his Introduction by saying that it would "justify" his procedure and diminish his readers' potential disappointments "to a just extent" (*auf ein billiges Mass*, mistranslated in

14. Steiner (1984, 10) perceptively remarks that the Dora case is probably the one "that most stimulated Freud's capacities as a writer. . . . The elusiveness of the story and of Dora's statements; the excitement, the triumph when Freud was discovering her unconscious phantasies and wishes and telling Dora the results of his discoveries; the particular mimetic, seductive capacity of Dora to please him and then to disappoint him by interrupting her analysis: all that seems to have transformed itself in the particular structure that the case has assumed and in the particular language Freud has used to write it."

the *Standard Edition* as "partly"—163/7). Asserting then that he can "escape reproach," he rhetorically asks whether he has to defend himself against reproach for speaking frankly with Dora; he even rallies behind another writer, Goethe, who railed against the reproachful spirit of his age.

Freud cites Goethe to forestall criticism about the length of his narrative, quoting him to the effect that not only science and art but also patience must be shown in a work (Freud's impatience with Dora violates that instruction). In the only footnote in the Introduction, affixed nearly twenty years later, Freud holds that no fair judge would reproach him for not having done more with the aborted therapy. In his "Postscript," Freud returns to the subject of being reproached by colleagues for proposing a psychological theory that ipso facto cannot solve a pathological problem.

Constantly using an adversarial stance toward Dora for reproaching him and others, Freud behaves just like her. And whereas he downplays the hostility that she got from adults around her, he readily reproaches his own readers for their hostility; he inveighs against ill-willed critics, prurient nonmedical and medical readers (8–9, 48–49, 50, 51), speculative philosophers, timid physicians, and critical "colleagues" (*Fachgenossen*, mistranslated in *S.E.* as "other specialists," 167/10).

The principal target of his reproaches, Dora threatened him much more than the Rat Man and the Wolf Man did (her case history has longer sections of emotive interchange). But unlike his other writings, the Dora case history possesses a minimum of self-irony, perhaps because Freud felt that he had been too much the butt of Dora's reproaches. His assertions gradually become more forceful and unnuanced, ironically glossing his characterization of the case as fragment, as partial truth. If Freud used dry language with his patient, he did not use calm language; he was stirred up and showed it in tones of irony, frustration, irritation, bitterness, vengeance, and self-indulgent triumph.

Like the helpless Dora, Freud experienced himself to be a commodity in a system of circulation, though of a far different kind. Being published made Freud feel vulnerable in the hands of the specialist and predominantly male reader; being read meant resembling an analysand, being a passive object, a woman. Freud struggled against that identification, against feeling passive with the reader and being mistreated by him. Thus, the advantages enjoyed by Freud the writer in his self-restorative and vindicative attempts to spite the absent, powerless Dora were undercut by his helplessness and possible castration at the hands of an absent, yet all-powerful, reader.

To counteract those identifications, Freud resorted to a variety of strategies, including satire. For instance, to control the spread of opposition, Freud kills two birds with one shot of irony: "Whereas before I was accused of giving *no* information about my patients, now I shall be accused of giving information about my patients which ought not to be given. I can only hope that in both cases the critics will be the same, and that they will merely have shifted the pretext for their reproaches" (7).

Another of Freud's strategies is to offer a metatheory of how his text should be read. He announces baldly that anyone disbelieving the sexual etiology of hysteria should suspend judgment of the case "until his own work has earned him the right to a conviction." He counsels readers to analyze their dreams to understand what he has to say. Collapsing the readers into his message, Freud proclaims that if they refuse to analyze their dreams, they would find bewilderment in his text and would project that feeling onto him. Yet, Freud wryly concludes, all neuroses are bewildering and cause bewilderment. In effect, Freud draws up a metatheory about interpreting his work because he knows that his ideal reader is not contemporaneous. On the Dora case he says: "One does one's duty and does not write for the day alone" (Freud, 1985, 433).

Freud's metatheory of reading brings us to the complex issue of aims. The protagonists in the Dora case history harbored diverse, evolving aims, conscious and unconscious. Whether those aims were fulfilled and how each person's aims were perceived by the others make up another story. In some ways the distinctive conscious aims of Freud were more complicated. As a clinician, scientific explorer, and case writer, he has interflowing purposes that continue to elicit a range of interpretations.

Freud the clinician emphasizes two coinciding aims of analysis: the practical one of removing symptoms by conscious thought and the "theoretical" (18) one of repairing the patient's memory. Freud strove not as much to heal as to apply his dream theory in the accomplishment of his aims. Because dreams avoided repression, they were privileged in his efforts to elucidate symptoms and fill in amnesia.[15] Hence he supplemented *The Interpretation of Dreams* by demonstrating through psychoanalytic treatment "the only practical application" (15) of dream interpretation: to discover other psychic phenomena. It is noteworthy that Freud drops the term "hysteria" from the original title of the case history and does not even use it in a chapter heading. Two chapters in the case are titularly devoted to "the first dream" and "the second dream," thereby highlighting a direct continuation with the classic Dreambook. He also meant to replace Breuer's theory about the etiological impact of hypnoid states by clarifying the role of psychic processes and organic determinants in the most common cases of hysteria, to show that sexuality with all its infantile roots furnishes the "drive-power" (*Triebkraft*, 278/115) behind every hysterical symptom, and to demonstrate the impact of bisexuality and masturbation on pathology. Through the cathartic vengeance and symbolic self-restoration in his gendered textuality, Freud offsets his prior frustrations, which include his inability to give a full explanation for Dora's *petite hystérie* (23) and his failure to effect a permanent cure of her symptoms and to have her marry Hans for the putative good of two unhappy ménages.

Freud's artful rhetoric balances the expository fragility of his case history and the incomplete fulfillment of his aims. Years after the termination of the Dora case, he made this self-critical reflection, which has been overlooked in the secondary literature: "Case histories could never serve—as Sadger thinks—as *introduc-*

---

15. Kanzer (1980, 72) writes that Freud had two aims. One was therapeutic but the more important was to apply his dream theory in the clinical situation.

tions. Furthermore, he fully agrees with Stekel that case histories that are not worked over are completely indigestible. A scrupulous but 'artistic' presentation, such as that of Dora's history, is the only acceptable possibility. In any event, the use of illustrations in this work should be sparing" (Nunberg and Federn, 1967, 213). The artistically managed pace of Freud's own exposition varies from a leisurely to rapid. In effect, the reader must be ever alert to follow Freud's feints, sudden modifications at unlikely turns, and assertions whose forcefulness covers up the lack of demonstration. Often we are liable to continue the momentum of Freud's line of thought and run past his quick swerve into an altering perspective.[16]

Let us restrict our rhetorical scrutiny to a sampling from Freud's "Prefatory Remarks." He opens with a sentence whose impressive length harmonizes with the ambitious aims and temporal scope of his treatise (unfortunately Strachey diminishes the majestic impact by dividing the one-sentence paragraph into three sentences—163/7). As Freud stresses a link with his past work shortly thereafter, he confirms and fine-tunes his previous findings about hysteria, yet renounces the method permitting those findings. He starts out by saying that he now will substantiate his previously published views on the genesis of hysterical symptoms and processes and give results that can be tested and checked; nevertheless, he admits, the analytic technique used at the time was "totally inadequate in dealing with the finer structure of a neurosis" (12). But his contemporary readers might have asked, What about the technique that he used with Dora—might that, too, be outmoded some day? To ward off that possible objection by his readership, Freud immediately claims that his superior technique is indeed the "only possible one" (12). In that arbitrary fashion he stakes out the ground rules for discussion: he will allow that his discovery of hysterical processes can be supple-

16. In the words of one eminent psychoanalytic critic of the Dora case, Freud's "artistic presentation enabled his ideas to prevail despite opposition" (Glenn, 1980, 4).

mented, but he insists on the unchangeability of his technical method. The great doubter and assailant of religious doctrine is here rising to promulgate with papal infallibility.

Addressing at this juncture the thorny problem of verifying his results, Freud rises to the rhetorical challenge. He maintains that by and large he will omit any account of his verifiable new technique except as it concerns dreams. But Freud is quick to clarify that he is not carried away by illusory hopes; *The Interpretation of Dreams*, the interim work between his *Studies on Hysteria* and the Dora case, had a bad reception even though objectors could easily have tested the technique of dream analysis. Rather than avoid the possibility of a repeatable historical defeat, Freud reasserts the way his text should be read, and adds that anyone reading it another way will fall victim to the snares of familiarization. If, for example, medical readers do not yield to such an investigative desideratum, they will be bewildered by the phenomena of neurosis, and their very familiarity with those phenomena will work to conceal their bewilderment from themselves (11).

Freud's literary artifice also appears in his ambivalent clinical reliance on literary terms. As if to underline the derivative character of his belletristic work, Freud calls attention to the artistry of psychic life itself: the connection between the symptom and its unconscious content is "clever and artful" (*geschickt und kunstvoll;* compare "clever tour de force" in *S.E.,* 200/41). We read, too, of Philip's "fairy tale" of his suicide (33), Dora's "comedy of suicide" (*Selbstmordkomödie,* roughly translated by Strachey as "pretence at suicide," 191n/33n), and the "fable of Oedipus" (*Ödipusfabel*), a "poetical rendering" of the sexual attraction between parents and children (56). Alluding to an unmarried woman, Freud speaks of her falling under the influence of an aunt's romance or a romantic novel (*Roman,* 183n/25n). He also claims to forsake the use of another literary genre: "I shall avoid writing a satire upon doctors and laymen pretending to respectability" (49). Upon referring to Schnitzler in a footnote, Freud asks readers to co-create: "Let us imagine" (203n/44n). After all this, we are not taken aback to find

Freud's typical denial that he is not "a man of letters" who can selectively represent reality in a short story; for the sake of the complete truth, Freud continues, he himself must include the theme of homosexuality, which effaces "the outlines of the fine poetic conflict" in Dora's life (59).

Alien to strict scientific discourse, Freud's punful repetition of lexical items contains a plot in itself. Again, as with the ambiguity of Freud's clinical references, Strachey often beclouds Freud's language. In one passage the English translation omits the sight imagery that subtly binds participants and observers. Dora says that she saw (*sehen*) in her cousin a "reflection" (*Spiegelung*; compare *Spiegel*, "mirror") of her own childhood, adding that the cousin was a "witness" (*Zeugin*) to parental quarreling; thereupon Freud declares that he usually "sees" (*sehen*, translated in *S.E.* as "regarding") such an association as confirming his theory (217/57). In another passage of visual imagery (201–202/42) we read that with her illness Dora had an aim "in view" (*im Auge*). Then Freud tells us in a parenthetical remark that readers should "see [*siehe*] her farewell letter" (the visual referent is omitted in *S.E.*). Next, Freud brings up how, revelatory of Philip's concern for her, tears could come "in his eyes" (*in die Augen*).

Freud also displays his playfulness in addressing the issue of discretion. For the subject of his case he chooses a person whose fate was not "played out" (*spielten*, 164/8) in Vienna; and he accepts the possibility that his case report might accidentally "fall" (literally, "play," *spielt*, 165/9) into Dora's hands. Elsewhere, Freud says that Dora's infantile wish to put her father into Hans's place had the potency (*Potenz*, 249/86) necessary for forming a dream—an ironical theoretical remark in the light of Philip's sexual impotence.

In a paragraph discussing how Dora transferentially identified him with Herr K., Freud concedes that he himself was not "master" (*Herr*) of the transference (282/118; translated in *S.E.* as "mastered"). Freud also calls attention to the meaning of *Verkehr* as both "traffic" and "sexual relations" (99n); keeping in mind its additional meaning as "social relationships," we can better appreciate the aftermath of Dora's condolence call on the Zellenkas when their daughter died in 1901. According to Freud's account, after Dora's visit she did not resume "relations" (*Verkehr*) with the K.'s, but about four months later she accidentally met Herr K. in a place where there was much traffic (*Verkehr*, 285/121). Strachey muffles a play between voice and silence in another sentence: "A very short time after she had tacitly accepted this explanation her cough vanished—which fitted in very well with my view." Being "tacitly" ill renders the German *stillschweigen*, literally, "still silent," which prepares the way for "fitted in," *stimmte*, whose substantival form, *Stimme*, means "voice" (207/48).

Special effects occur in what is perhaps the most quoted passage in the case, one that anticipates Freud's all-crucial observation about the hands of Moses sculpted by Michelangelo: "He that has eyes to see and ears to hear may convince himself that no mortal can keep a secret. If his lips are silent, he chatters with his finger-tips; betrayal oozes out of him at every pore" (77–78). Critics have rightly pointed out the biblical tone of this passage, yet they have not heeded that the "oozing" anticipates the ensuing paragraph about catarrh; like "catharsis," the term "catarrh" comes from the Greek *katarhein*, "to flow down."

Sometimes it seems as if sounds and words circulate in Freud's preconscious, remaining active there and ready to emerge in echoic repetitions or in clusters. After stating that the "shell of Venus" (*der Venusmuschel*, 240/77) stands for the female genitals, Freud speaks of the physical irritation in Dora's throat as acting like a grain of sand that will be surrounded by nacre made by the oyster (*Muscheltier*, literally, "shell animal," 245/83). The following example of manual allusions starts at the end of one paragraph and continues into the next (I quote from Strachey's translation except where indicated).

> [Through her illness Dora had] a powerful weapon . . . in her hands [*in Händen*] . . . [motives] are not present [*vorhanden*, that is, "at hand"] in the beginning of illness. . . . Their presence [*Vorhandensein*] can be reckoned upon in every case . . . to begin with there is no use to which it [a symptom] can be put in the

psychic household [*psychischen Haushalt*; compare "domestic economy of the mind" in *S.E.*]; . . . some psychical current . . . finds it convenient to make use of it. . . . Let us imagine a workman, a roofer [*Dachdecker*; compare "bricklayer" in *S.E.*), who has fallen and become crippled and now earns his livelihood by begging at the street corner . . . he has in the meantime forgotten his handicraft [*Handwerk*; compare "trade" in *S.E.*]. (202–203/42–44)

The chapter on the second dream affords some interesting examples of Strachey's lexical apartheid policy whereby he obliterates Freud's democratic thrust to blend theoretical and concrete language. Freud's repetition of lexical items, moreover, fades out in English. The relevant passage about Dora in the Dresden gallery is striking in the oneiric bind between Dora's dreamy life-state, the process of her nightdream, and Freud's own reflection in the present tense (put into the past in *S.E.*): "She passed two hours before the *Sistina* in a quiet, dreamy [*träumender*; "rapt" in *S.E.*] admiration. . . . It is most certain that these associations really belong to the material forming the dream [*traumbildenden*]. . . . I notice already that "pictures" correspond to a nodal point in the fabric of the dream-thoughts. . . . But above all I see [compare "it was most evident" in *S.E.*] that she identifies with a young man in this first part of the dream" (259/96, my translation).

Two shorter examples of wordplay are worth mentioning. After referring to the dream segment where Dora "wanders [*irrt*] alone in a strange town" (258/95), Freud wonders whether a certain supposition in his dream commentary will make us "wander or go astray" (*gehen wir irre*, 260/98). Several pages later, we enjoy another verbal echoing. After Dora "opened" (*antreten*) the third session, Freud said, "You know that you are free to stop [*austreten*] the treatment at any time" (268/105). Of a different aesthetic nature is Freud's explanation of components in Dora's second dream. In explaining two components, Freud mentions his later analysis of the third and most important component (100n); then he makes readers wait to discover the third component, which is none other than the theme of waiting. In a more striking way Freud repeats this narrative mimesis in the Wolf Man case history.[17]

Of a different discursive order is Freud's description of Dora's first asthma attack, which occurred during her father's absence. Freud fittingly writes up the core of his epical reconstruction in a very lengthy sentence. Reading it aloud and without stop, the reader is liable to fall short of breath, thus enacting the discomfort visiting the eight-year-old mountain climber: "To this was added the thought that her father was forbidden to climb mountains and was not allowed to over-exert himself, because he suffered from shortness of breath; then came the recollection of how much he had exerted himself with her mother that night, and the question whether it might not have done him harm; next came concern whether *she* might not have over-exerted herself in masturbating—an act which, like the other, led to a sexual orgasm accompanied by a slight dyspnoea—and finally came a return of the dyspnoea in an intensified form as a symptom" (243/80). The performative aspect of the passage exemplifies the multileveled richness characterizing Freud's prose.

17. In the French edition of my book on the Wolf Man (Mahony, 1995), a considerable revision of the English version (1984), I did not alter anything in the following passage, quoted from the English version (90): "Previously in his case history Freud merely hinted at the way his patient had 'interrupted the primal scene' (Freud, 1918, 38) but reserved, saved up (*ausparte, G.W.,* 12:89/*S.E.,* 17:59) its elaboration for later on. That later on occurs when Freud is expatiating on the Wolf Man's anal symptoms, his longstanding constipation, and his orientation to money and faeces. Indicating that one portion of the primal scene has been kept back (*zurückgehalten*), Freud declares that he is now ready to *produce* it. But the English 'produce' is a woeful translation of the German *nachtragen.* . . . [B]esides being a nodal word, it carries the anally economic meaning of 'to pay up arrears,' thus being a deferred reaction to *ausparte,* or 'saved up.' And what hint has Freud retained all this time? None other than 'the child finally interrupted his parents' intercourse by passing a stool, which gave him an excuse for screaming.' Such was Freud's construction of a 'concluding act' (there is a definite theatrical note in the German *Schlussakt*). And how did the patient react to this construction? He confirmed it by staging sound effects, by producing 'transitory symptoms' (80). In effect, the analyst and patient were locked in a quid pro quo of anal retention and release extending from the clinical setting to the pages of the deferred expository narrative."

Of great significance in Freud's verbal practice is the confluence of his theorization, textuality, and corporeal fantasy of Dora as flowing liquid (did traces of that appear in the calligraphy of the Dora manuscript?). For page after page, references to liquids overflow Freud's text. Given the decisive presence of Fliess in the case, I suggest that the frequent mention of liquids is overdetermined by virtue of his name (*fliessen,* "to flow") and even that of Freud's adolescent beloved, Gisela Fluss ("river"), who was the secret subject of an anonymous essay that Freud had written shortly before (1899).

Freud held that in the intention to flee Hans's sexual harassment Dora wanted her father's protection against her sexual desires and their dangerous, wet results. Embedded in Freud's fantasy, Dora is afflicted with disgusting secretions of genital discharge, dangerous liquids of sexual excitement, unpredictable associative currents. Mental currents flow to the symptom like new wine into old bottles (54); a blocked libido flows back onto its old riverbed (*Strombett;* compare "channel" in *S.E.,* 242/79). Indicative of the motive forces leading to the formation of symptoms, "a stream of water which meets with an obstacle in the river-bed is dammed up and flows back into old channels, which had formerly seemed fated to run dry" (51).

The physical and mental operate as crosscurrents. Genital disorders tend to infuse (*einzuflössen;* compare "inspire" in *S.E.*) women with repugnance; and an abnormal vaginal secretion causes disgust (247/84). As a sick little girl, Dora saw her parents' love "streaming toward" her (*zuströmt;* compare "is lavished" in *S.E.,* 204/44). Dora felt that she was afflicted with a disgusting discharge (*Ausflusse,* literally, "outflow"), a leucorrhea (*fluor albus,* "a white flowing," 247/84). Her dream carried a mental current and a contrary "current" (*Strömung,* 248/85; see also 220/60, 222/62, 223/63). According to one "current of feeling" (*Gefühlsströmmung,* 252/89), her father protected against dangerous wetness, "a liquid something" (*etwas Flüssiges,* 253/90); the jewel case was a compromise between two mental currents (92). During treatment, the patient's report is at first like an unnavigable river whose "bed" (*Bett*; compare "stream" in *S.E.*) is sometimes choked; later on, the report may run shallow (*seicht*; Strachey, "dry") and leave gaps unfilled (173–174/16). In the beginning of Dora's treatment, the material had not yet run "dry" (*verseigte*, 283/119). Freud—I might repeat—as an adolescent kept a journal in Greek and as an adult could cite classical Greek passages, so he was certainly aware of the etymological presence of *rhein*, "to flow," in his many references to catarrh (and one to gonorrhea, 238/75).[18]

Another intriguing part of Freud's textuality portrays how he and Dora are bound up in a constellation of references dealing with dryness and excitement (208–209/48–49). Ideally, associative material should flow, but the current must be shored up by correct medical standards. After bringing up the "tickling" (*Kitzel*) in Dora's throat as an "exciting stimulus" (*Reizanlass*), Freud expresses hope that his account will not "excite" (*erregt*) medical readers. Freud insists that he talks in a "dry" (*trockene*) way about sexuality to patients who may not be "open" in the beginning. "J'appelle un chat un chat," he adds. Then he rails against those who think that his analytic method must give him "titillation" (*Kitzel*, 208/48). The whole passage becomes even richer when we recall that "clitoris" in German is *Kitzler*, "tickler," and that Freud focuses on a fantasy of fellatio rather than cunnilingus. He knows that the latter is "faire la minette" in French (Freud, 1909, 283), the literal meaning of *minette* being "little female cat". It is impossible to determine at this point whether Freud was aware that his language was influenced by the nickname that Fliess and his wife called each other: "kitten" (*Katzel*; Freud, 1985, 237).

Like his daughter, Philip figures in an overdetermined latent verbal pattern throughout the case history. One critic has observed that the pen name sometimes used by Otto Bauer was Weber

---

18. There is even a suggestion of liquidity in the marital "solution" (*Lösung*) that Freud related to Dora: "Indeed, if your temptation at L—— had had a different upshot, this would have been the only possible solution for all parties concerned" (271/108). A similar, though more powerful, use of "solution" figures in Freud's Irma dream.

(weaver), a choice motivated by his father's textile mills.[19] German readers will be alert to the whole cloth of Freud's expository comments—for instance, where he speaks of an associative "web" (*Gespinst*; compare "chain" in *S.E.*, 166/10) and mentions how dream interpretation is "patched" (*einflicht*; compare "woven" in *S.E.*, 167/10) into a case history. In the course of treatment a symptom is "woven" (*verflochten*, 169/12) into various contexts. Dreams are "spun out" (*ausgesponnenen*) between the symptom and the pathogenic idea (172/15). We are exhorted to note the "weaving" (*Einflechtung*; compare "worked into" in *S.E.*, 225/64) of Dora's first dream into the analysis as a whole. Dora's second dream has a fabric (*Gewebe*; compare "network" in *S.E.*, 259/96) of nodal points.

Pertinently, Freud first used of the term "psychical coating" (*psychische Umkleidung*) in the Dora case (83, 84, 99n); he used it only once afterward (1912, 248). Dora's reproaches were (*unterfüttert*) or doubled (*doubliert*, 194/35–36; note that Freud doubled by using synonyms). Freud exposed Dora's preoccupation with the Zellenka children as a cloak (*Deckmantel*, 196/37). Etymology in this context helps us to perceive that in more ways than one Freud's textuality is subtle. It enriches our appreciation to recall that the word "text" comes from the Latin *textare*, "to weave," and "subtle" from *sub textare*, "to weave under"; the unpronounced *b* of "subtle," gone with the wind, bespeaks the whole. Freud plays out those relations on the field of textuality. The etymological serendipity of *textare* also bears witness to Freud's kinship throughout his imagistic subtext with Herr Bauer's textile entrepreneurship.

Freud's repetition of sounds, a cardinal feature of his textuality, shows him as a poet who writes with his ear and employs sounds with the force of copulative verbs to establish new semantic configurations. The following example of Freud's phonic copula appears in an interpretation that he gives to Dora: "At the moment when Herr K. used the words 'I get nothing out of my

19. See Rogow, 1979, 247n.

wife'—which were the same words he used [*gesagt*] to the governess—fresh emotions were aroused [*wachgerufen*] in you and tipped the balance [*Wagschale*]. 'Does he dare [*wagt*],' you said to yourself, 'to treat me like a governess, like a servant?' " (269/106). A similar phonic element effects a latent relation common to *gesagt, wachgerufen, Wagschale,* and *wagt;* technically, although the *g* is a stop or continuant and the *ch* a fricative, both are velar and voiceless. Here Freud, the poetic listener to his own impulses, weaves into one fabric Dora, the governess, affective equilibrium, and words of seduction and offense.

A more spectacular instance of Freud's subtle phonic artifice is contained in his explanation of the principle of contiguity, whereby *a* and *b* placed side by side become *ab.* In the German text of his explanation, Freud uses such words as *Abwechslung, Abhängigkeit, Abwesenheit, Abneigung,* which, by virtue of their prefix, become more or less synonymous. My bracketed additions to the translation in the *Standard Edition* highlight Freud's preconscious activity.

> Dora suddenly brought in an allusion to her own alternations [*Abwechslung*] between good and bad health during the first years of her girlhood at B——; and I was thus driven to suspect that her states of health were to be regarded as depending [*Abhängigkeit*] upon something else, in the same way as Frau K.'s. (It is a rule of psychoanalytic technique that an internal connection which is still undisclosed will announce its presence by means of a contiguity—a temporal proximity—of associations; just as in writing, if 'a' and 'b' are put side by side, it means that the syllable 'ab' is to be formed out of them). Dora had had a very large number of attacks of coughing accompanied by loss of voice. Could it be that the presence or absence [*Abwesenheit*] of the man she loved had had an influence upon the appearance and disappearance of the symptoms of her illness? . . . Her illness was therefore a demonstration of her love for K., just as his wife's was a demonstration of her *dislike* [*Abneigung*]. (198/39)

The study of Freud's preconscious is in its infancy. I venture that his syntactic and phonic patterns will be the target of revolutionary computerized studies in the next century.

Another aspect of Freud's style worth mentioning is his vivid use of the present tense. Not only in Dora's dreams, already discussed, does Strachey displace Freud's present tense into the past; he deadens the vividness of the present elsewhere, too. Through his grammatical present, Freud achieves more than dramatic impact; he renders intrapsychic activity in its immediacy and simultaneously establishes greater closeness with his audience. Here is Freud restored in his immediacy.

> A similar and very amusing incident has happened to me recently. In the middle of a session an older lady takes out a small ivory box, apparently to refresh herself with a candy; she tries to open it, then hands it to me so that I'll convince myself how hard it is to open. I utter my suspicion that this box must mean something special; I see it today [*heute*, omitted in *S.E.*], indeed for the first time, although its owner has been already seeing me for more than a year. (*G.W.*, 5:240, my translation)

And here is Strachey's Freud:

> A very entertaining episode of a similar kind occurred to me a short time ago. In the middle of a session the patient—a lady who was no longer young—brought out a small ivory box, ostensibly in order to refresh herself with a sweet. She made some efforts to open it, and then handed it to me so that I might convince myself how hard it was to open. I expressed my suspicion that the box must mean something special, for this was the very first time I had seen it, although its owner had been coming to me for more than a year. (77)

Perhaps the distance effected by Strachey in his translation stems from the social archness in his aristocratic upbringing. Let it be said, in any case, that a psychoanalysis of his translation and its impact on the theory of a conflict-free ego has yet to be written.

A consideration of the writing in the Dora case would not be complete without a review of the historical complications bearing on its composition and publication. In a letter to Fliess on October 14, 1900, Freud alludes to writing *Psychopathology of Everyday Life* and "On Dreams" and mentions Dora for the first time. He set about writing up the Dora case in January 1901 and finished the other two texts afterward. Freud's hyperinvestment in the Dora case also manifested itself in a series of memory lapses. Twice in the note appended to the Dora case in 1923 (13–14) and twice in the "History of the Psychoanalytic Movement" (1914), Freud misdates the treatment, placing it in 1899 instead of 1900. This chronological error put the Dora case within the period when Freud was close to Fliess, whose moral support he needed for the publication of *The Interpretation of Dreams*; in his mind, Freud thus moved Dora herself under the aegis of Fliess. But the misdating also returned Freud to the pre-Achensee period, to the time when he mistook the theory of bisexuality for his own; in that way, he also moved to make Dora his own, to (re)cover her. In a blundering commentary, Jones offers that Freud's error arose from a "connection in his mind between the essay and *The Interpretation of Dreams* (which the publisher also misdated by a year), since it had closely corresponded with the chapter of the same title he had intended to insert in that book. Dora had in fact arrived a year [1900] or two [1901] after this time" (1953, 363; compare 1955, 255). With the 1901 date Jones repeats Freud's timing error of a year, but in the other direction.

Another explanation of Freud's mistake concerns the temporal proximity between Dora's treatment and his conversation with Fliess about bisexuality that took place in the summer of 1900. As reported in *The Psychopathology of Everyday Life*, that conversation involved a significant memory lapse on Freud's part. He admitted wishing to negate Fliess's priority in recognizing the psychological role of bisexuality. I would add that the ramifications of the subject of bisexuality determined Freud's parapraxis as well. Dora's real first name was Ida, the same as that of Fliess's wife; additionally, in her paranoid reactions of jealousy she reminded Freud of both Fliess and his wife. Freud felt in particular that through her jealousy Ida Fliess actively opposed his intimate friendship with her husband (Freud, 1985, 447; compare 196–197n in the same volume).

There are a number of other discrepancies in Freud's assertions about writing and publishing the Dora case. Although he was irritated by Dora's leaving him after nearly three months instead of the year he had promised for full recovery, to some degree his irritation was mitigated by an irreplaceable bonus. Did he not say in his "Prefatory Remarks" that he knew how to write up three months' worth of material but not a year's worth (11)? In his "Postscript," too, Freud spoke of the "great merit" of the case; that is, "the unusual clarity which makes it seem so suitable as a first introductory publication is closely bound up with its great defect, which led to its being broken off prematurely" (118).

For another—and here I must elaborate an assertion made early in this book—in spite of Freud's public claim that only one physician, whom Strachey presumed to be Fliess, knew that Dora was his patient (8), another doctor knew: Oscar Rie, Fliess's brother-in-law (Freud, 1985, 438, 447). Rie was a secondary but not negligible audience. Freud recalled that he had known Rie for forty-five years and that they had "shared everything for a generation and a half."[20] Besides being a pediatrician to Freud's children, Rie played cards with him and worked with him as coauthor of a 220-page manuscript on children's palsy in 1891. Later Rie became the butt of Freud's Irma dream for having criticized Freud's treatment of her. Still later, he objected to Freud's interpretation of *Hamlet* (Freud, 1985, 381). Who else could claim to be Freud's most immediate audience for the Irma dream, the oedipal interpretation of *Hamlet*, and the Dora case? We read with disbelief, therefore, Freud's complaint that he lost his "*last* audience" upon his split with Fliess (Freud, 1985, 456).

Freud also made this disingenuous and self-mythologizing claim: "My *Interpretations of Dreams* and my 'Fragment of an Analysis of a Case of Hysteria' [the case of Dora] were suppressed by me—if not for the nine years enjoined by Horace—at all events

20. Letter of September 18, 1931, to M. Bonaparte (Schur, 1972, 430).

for four or five years before I allowed them to be published. . . . I was the only worker in a new field, so that my reticence involved no danger to myself and no loss to others" (1925, 248–249). This statement flies in the face of Freud's unpublicized efforts to publish the case in the months after it was finished. Those efforts, traceable in his correspondence with Fliess, may be summarized as follows. On January 14, 1901, Freud declared that he was writing *Psychopathology of Everyday Life* and "Dreams and Analysis: A Fragment of an Analysis." Eleven days later, Freud stated that he had finished "Dreams and Hysteria" the previous day and that Theodor Ziehen, coeditor with Carl Wernicke of *Monatsschrift für Psychiatrie und Neurologie* and, oddly enough, a staunch opponent of psychoanalysis, had already accepted it (obviously in some communication prior to the completion of the article being finished on January 24).

Whether Freud actually wrote the case in three weeks or so is insignificant. What matters is that in his memory he composed it "during the two weeks immediately following" the end of Dora's treatment (13n). Thus, I contend, his writing was an anniversary reaction to the two weeks' decision taken by Dora to quit and the two weeks it took her talk to her mother about the lakeside trauma. Freud lived with the case for two weeks while writing it, then finished it, discharged it, wrote it off. He overlooked that he had been the maid whom Dora had discharged on a decision made two weeks earlier. During the write-up, he unconsciously and vindictively was a boss who had discharged Dora as a maid. Accordingly, Freud had three salient reactive experiences after the treatment: his belated discoveries of transference and bisexuality and his countertransferential identification with being a maid. In more ways than one, composing the case was a writing throughout.

On February 15, Freud wrote to Fliess that in the next few days he expected to finish the *Psychopathology of Everyday Life,* and then correct it and the Dora case, and send them off. Then, it seems, Freud began to blow hot and cold about the possibility of clinical indiscretion. But by March 3 he had shown his case notes

to Oscar Rie, who gave them a cold reception. Freud was nonetheless inclined to publish: "I have just completed the second
treatise [Dora], shall be able to correct and patch up both of them
during the coming weeks, and shall then attend to arranging
simultaneous publishing. At his request I let Oscar read 'Dreams
and Hysteria,' but I derived little joy from it. I shall make no
further attempt to break through my isolation" (Freud, 1985,
438).

More time elapsed—a considerable time for Freud's fluent
pen and an indication of his serious vacillation. On May 8, Freud
confessed, "I have not yet made up my mind to send off" the Dora
essay. Finally, on June 9 he announced that " 'Dreams and Hysteria' has been [sent] off, and will probably not come to the
attention of an astounded public until fall" (Freud, 1985, 441,
442).

The other relevant fact for 1901 is that sometime during that
year Freud decided to submit the Dora essay to Korbinian Brodmann, editor of the *Journal für Psychologie und Neurologie*, who
rejected it (Freud, 1993b, 39). Jones (1955, 256) speculates that
after Ziehen and Wernicke had provisionally accepted the case,
Freud had doubts about whether they would approve the finished
product because of its indiscretions; and in order not to jeopardize
Ziehen and Wernicke's acceptance of *Psychopathology of Everyday
Life*, sometime between January and June he sent his case history
to Brodmann as a security measure. According to Jones, after
Psychopathology of Everyday Life was in press and after Brodmann
turned down the manuscript of the Dora case, Freud sent it to
Ziehen, who did object to its indiscretions.

The more likely chain of events, I propose, is that *after* Ziehen
voiced his reserve, Freud tried Brodmann, who then uttered an
outright outright rejection. The weight of the two disapprovals,
plus Fliess's and Rie's attitudes toward either him or his manuscript, at last moved Freud to shelve the work. I wonder, in
addition, whether Freud's hesitation was also due to having Hans
or his wife in treatment during his write-up. We notice in the case
history that whereas Freud criticizes both of Dora's parents, he

spares Hans at every turn and resorts to a mythological allusion in his single criticism of Peppina.

A final, not fully answerable question concerns the reason that Freud rushed to write up the case. No mistake about it, Freud already had a history of rushing unfounded professional claims into print. For example, he successfully urged the reluctant Breuer to publish the Anna O. case history; both men colluded to suppress the information that at the end of her treatment she not only still had her former symptoms but had developed new ones. Years later, Freud boasted in his essay "Sexual Aetiology of the Neuroses" (1898, 107): "I have in recent years almost worked a therapeutic procedure which I propose to describe as psychoanalytic. I owe a great number of successes to it"; yet in a contemporary letter to Fliess, Freud lamented his continuing lack of success in finishing a single analytic case (Mahony, 1994).

Freud's haste to write up the Dora case was motivated by its superiority to his few longer and completed cases at the time. Not only did the young patient spend most of her life outside Vienna, therefore posing fewer problems of confidentiality, but she had also supplied him with crucial oneiric material. He therefore interrupted writing *Psychopathology of Everyday Life* to write the Dora case history, which, together with the complementary *Studies on Hysteria* and *The Interpretation of Dreams,* constitute a trilogy that would be cited without end.

6

Conclusions

Dora's case history exemplifies a remarkable amount of coercion. A male adult forced himself upon a young female who afterward was forced by her father into therapy sessions where the therapist elected to force or "direct" (32) her associations, the pursuit of his own theories perforce interfering with his free-floating attention. Freud built gratuitous reconstructions, projecting onto the young Dora his own excitability and wishes for her excitation and corralling her desires within the orbit of his knowledge and ambitions. Failing in common sense and common decency, he dismissed much of the victim's complaint but praised the attacker. Freud had neither respect nor sympathy for Dora.

I do not feel that Dora became capable of that gentle sadness that comes from calm remove in face of the inevitable disappointments in life and the necessary death of certain youthful idealisms. The abatement of Dora's symptoms, which were neither permanent nor generalized, could have stemmed from her triumph over one more male doctor. Yet her victories over the phallocratic plans for her sexual union were, I suspect, Pyrrhic ones that sapped her ability to lead a happy life. She never had a chance to resolve her sexual guilt—not in Freud's intended sense but in the sense of a victim's enmeshment.

Dora comes across in Freud's text as vindictive rather than self-vindicating. To Freud, her intelligence came from her father, but her vengeance was all her own. The fifteen-year-old, though traumatized by the sexual attack of a much older man, should have acted differently at the lake; the young woman should have yielded to Freud's pressuring and married her pursuer. Freud might have asked, What does the woman want? More to the point, he should have asked, What does the woman in me want? We cannot excuse Freud's comportment by invoking his ignorance of countertransferential awareness or the general state of psychoanalytic theory and practice at the time. Freud himself attacked his medical contemporaries for rejecting the notion of infantile sexuality. He wryly charged that they had only to draw on the "non-scientific" observation and wisdom of the nurses around them. Continuing Freud's line of argumentation, we might say that he needed only to emulate the behavior of a decent parent at the end of the nineteenth century in order to avoid launching indecent criticisms at Dora.

Although browbeaten by Freud, Dora did not completely succumb. Shortly after she left treatment, Freud was collecting his clinical cases to establish the link between neurosis and sexual life; he reported having but six cases, and they were "not the best" (Freud, 1985, 436). It is not certain how he judged the Dora case with reference to that less-than-ideal probative collection. It is certain, however, that Dora resisted Freud, confronted him, frustrated him. Students of psychoanalytic history often refer to the "conquistadorial nature" (*Conquistadorentemperament*) that Freud asserted in the beginning of 1900. At the end of that year, however, the self-styled conquistador (1985, 398) was stymied, let us say, by a conquistadora.

Something else eluded Freud, a factor hinted at by the vacillation in his developmental appellations for Dora. More than a mere rebellious adolescent, she identified in varying degrees with her father, mother, Peppina, and Hans in their personal aspirations as well as their objectal desires. Signs of the benevolent mother in Dora's experience appear in her care for her debilitated father and in her enrapturement with Peppina's "adorable" body and Raphael's Madonna. Dora also identified with the powerful destructive woman who could undermine her father's life with venereal disease, seduce her father and win his affections, and mock and defeat one male doctor after another. The all-powerful benevolent and malevolent mother contrasted with the defective Dora, who identified with the sick females around her. The kinds of women engaged Freud in ways beyond his reckoning. He was forever plagued by the woman inside him; he came fresh from the Dreambook, in which he contended on the field of symbolic inscription with the oedipal and more powerful preoedipal mother; and he concurrently suffered because of his dying friendship with Fliess. The elusive Dora was also an allegorical Everywoman, the eternal woman who engaged Freud for a lifetime in a changing configuration of desire, knowledge, and power.

Dora stood more still more. We recall that in Freud's mind, the Dora case represented the belated "unborn piece" of *The Interpretation of Dreams*, whose honored "godfather" was Fliess. We recall, too, that in spite of Freud's concurrent clinical focus on bisexuality, he did not address that issue with Dora. Clearly Freud's own feminine identity and castration complex were fueled in his conflictually interrelated associations with Fliess and with Dora. Another indication of her overdetermined significance is that she bore the same first name as Fliess's wife, and like her, she was accused by Freud of pernicious jealousy. Last, in Chapter 5, I brought up the ambivalent implications of Freud's misdating of the case, and I asked whether the affectionate name "kitten" which Fliess and his wife called each other influenced Freud's feline reference in the case history.

The treatment did have its positive side, which I will touch on again: Dora did receive some validation of what she had suffered, she did manage to go on and marry, she did learn the history of her desire, which had left aches throughout her body in verbalizable meanings. It was, moreover, a certain sign of health that Dora left Freud, for she did not want to be abused any longer or coopted into his phallocratic marital solution. During the treatment he gave anything but adequate attention to Dora's relationships with women, half of humanity. She spared herself further damage and—quite secondarily—spared psychoanalysis, too. Yet her abuse in the Italian mountain chain, recycled in a Viennese consulting room, was then repeated for decades in private reading rooms throughout the world. The fathers' misinterpretations were visited upon their children and their children's children. Freud was more unsettled than he knew. The medley of defeat and victory that each member of the therapeutic dyad experienced during the treatment assumed a new version in Freud's write-up. The dubiety of his etiological explanations of Dora's trauma and symptoms, the tendentious and often reckless interpretations of her dreams, the absence of transferential interpretation, the failure to integrate Dora's gynecophilic strivings— her deepest psychic current—into the interpreted material—all this adds up to a textual corpus that is as unhealthy as the body of Dora.

Freud said that if his published case should fall into Dora's hands, "she will learn nothing from it that she does not already know" (9). Not true. She would have found out about her gynecophilia and transferential ramifications—all-significant dynamic factors that Freud confessed to have discovered only subsequent to the treatment. And she might have relearned some insights that she repressed. Indeed, his denials rank among the most self-contradictory in the whole history of psychoanalysis and compete with Jones's boast in his three-volume hagiography that he had surmounted his "hero-worshipping propensities" *before* he met Freud (1953, xiii) and, necessarily, before he himself underwent any psychoanalytic treatment.[1]

Dora might have found it traumatic to read Freud's insistent depiction of her as mean and revengeful; she would have also

---

1. Jones's boast flies in the face of his avowal, found in his correspondence with Freud, which he reread in preparing the biography. In the letter of June 25, 1913, Jones admits: "My analysis [with Ferenczi] is giving me more self-dependence and freedom by diminishing further what was left of my father-complex, and I think you will welcome that as much as I do. It is better to have a natural and therefore permanent attitude of respect and admiration than a kind of veneration which brings with it the dangers of ambivalency" (Freud, 1993, 206). Compare Jones's letter of December 18, 1909 (Freud, 1993, 34).

learned about Freud's scientific belief—which he had purposely hidden from her—that the children of syphilitics were especially predisposed to severe neuropsychosis (compare 9 and 75). In claiming that Dora would not discover anything new by reading the case history, Freud represses the very notion of repeatable repression.

Although Freud was hostile to Dora, her voice and aphonia broke through his textual barrier and became a subtext. Freud's hyperinvested manifest text also evinces a faltering mastery. The factual distortions in Freud's "Prefatory Remarks," discussed earlier, throw light on the contradictions between the public and private Freud (I skip the further prevarications that characterize the different private Freuds).[2] We recall, too, that he continually attributes a wrong age to Dora, and he misdates the publication of the case four times. On the level of theoretical achievement, however, Freud appears in a new light. Many of his spectacular theories arose from unsuccessful cases, and in this case he learned more from Dora than she from him. In her case history we come upon seeds of psychoanalytic knowledge that would flower afterward in Freud's scientific development—aggression, narcissism, transference, defense organization, libidinal development, oedipal configurations, moral inhibitions, and the theory of analytic technique.

2. I am grateful to Haynal (1994) for the following examples of the self-contradictory private Freuds: (1) On the same day that Freud told Jung that he had "every advantage" over Abraham, Freud told Abraham that, compared with Jung, "you are closer to my intellectual constitution because of racial kinship" (cf. Freud and Abraham, 1965, letter of May 3, 1908, 34; and Freud and Jung, 1974, 146); and (2) In an unpublished letter of July 5, 1927, to Ferenczi, Freud confided, "I guess that J[ones] will make difficulties concerning your presidency," and added, "I absolutely do not want Jones to become president" of the International Psychoanalytic Association. Freud's letter of December 31, 1929, to Ferenczi repeated the same message. In a missive of July 30, 1930, Freud affirmed to Ferenczi that he wanted no one else but Ferenczi, as president, to deliver the speech at his grave. But lo and behold, Freud sent off a letter to Jones on September 12, 1932, congratulating him on his appointment as president and claiming that "there was not a moment's doubt that only you have the competence for leadership" (Freud and Jones, 1993, 708).

In spite of being the target of Freud's vengeance in his case history, Dora also reaped the benefit of fame from it. She became bizarrely proud of her therapeutic experience. Even though uncured she remained faithful to Freud—at least from Deutsch's point of view. The Wolf Man, too, derived substantial benefit from his patienthood; many years after Freud died, the Russian would still pick up the ringing phone and immediately blurt, "The Wolf Man speaking." With Dora and the Wolf Man we have, in effect, the beginnings of a new association of preoedipal and oedipal wrecks who find solace in being presented in painful narratives. Sometimes lonely people, gnawed by their own pain, will accept public humiliation as a way of getting company.

Freud's bitter reaction in his write-up and to its subsequent reception constitutes an organizing experience not only in his clinical career but also in the history of psychoanalysis. For decades during and after Freud's lifetime, analysts typically reacted to his case history with dutiful and outright praise that continued and even intensified Dora's victimization. The eulogistic commentary hailed her case as classic. But the lack of free association and transferential interpretation, the sine qua non of psychoanalytic treatment, disqualifies all previous attempts to classify Dora's therapy as such. If the founder of psychoanalysis conducted some non-analytic or anti-analytic treatment, so be it. To call the case history psychoanalytic or, worse yet, classic psychoanalysis is to indulge in terminological abuse, and we saw enough abuse of all kinds in the Dora case.

The case of Dora has an array of negative distinctions. It is one of the great psychotherapeutic disasters; one of the most remarkable exhibitions of a clinician's published rejection of his patient; spectacular, though tragic, evidence of sexual abuse of a young girl, and her own analyst's published exoneration of that abuse; an eminent case of forced associations, forced remembering, and perhaps several forced dreams (64), forced remembering of dreams, even forced remembering of forced dreams. Without any stretch of the imagination the case, the published history, and the subsequent reception can be called an example of continued

sexual abuse. Dora had been traumatized, and Freud retrauma-
tized her. And for roughly half a century the psychoanalytic community remained either collusively silent about that abuse or,
because of blind adoration, simply ignorant of it. Earlier in this
century psychoanalysis took a militant atheistic stance that was
ironically combined with a cult of hero worship and practices of
excommunication. Such an ambivalent compromise prompts me
to think that rigidly controlled institutions may marginalize courage in favor of individual dependence and its manifestations—
idealization, castration, and self-castration.

Either within or outside analysis, courage is a rare attainment. Cowardice is easily rationalized as prudence, but it is hard
to pretend to courage. If individuals eventually summon up the
courage to undergo analysis and join an organization of analyzed
people, their oedipal problems (which, we know, are never fully
resolved) tend to become activated and frequently to dampen
courage, with disastrous results. As Nietzsche explains in his preface to *Ecce Homo* (1954): "Error is cowardice. . . . Every conquest,
all progress in knowledge, is the result of courage, of hardness
towards one's self, of cleanliness towards one's self." Impeding the
progress of psychoanalysis alone, the erroneous, idealizing, and
hagiographical reactions to Freud constitute a boring yet pitiful
story. It is my firm conviction, however, that despite his foibles
and despite his diverse misdeeds (which must be recognized and
addressed), Freud does not need idealizing protection: he is great
enough to stand on his own. Any number of his writings, but
certainly not the Dora case, testify to his overall greatness.

All too often, the history of organized psychoanalysis reflects
a deep lack of courageous public expression, which Freud attributed to the dynamics of group psychology: "We have an impression of a state in which an individual's private emotional
impulses and intellectual acts are too weak to come to anything by
themselves and are entirely dependent for this on being reinforced
by being repeated in a similar way in the other members of the
group. We are reminded of how many of these phenomena of
dependence are part of the normal constitution of human society,

of how *little originality and personal courage* are found in it, of how much every individual is ruled by those attitudes of the group mind" (1921, 117, my italics). Freud's remarks are borne out by the traumatic impact that his disagreement with Ferenczi about technique had on the psychoanalytic world. For some time after Ferenczi died, analysts were reluctant to discuss issues of transference, countertransference, and regression.[3] Likewise, the editor in chief of the *International Journal of Psychoanalysis* found that analysts were wont to avoid dissenting from the theories of the awesome father Freud: "To challenge Freud's theories has usually been responded to with anxiety, as if a sacrilegious outrage were being perpetuated."[4]

Because the organizational pressures experienced by psychoanalysts do not obtain with nonanalytic readers, why did they initially abstain from criticizing Freud's case histories, in particular the one on Dora? Perhaps a good deal of the answer lies in the fateful lesson of charismatic public figures who spellbind a few generations and who, in a subsequent age, are subjected to a critical, collective transferential readjustment. Easier to explain is the recent abundance of protest against the Dora case that has come from the requestioning of countertransference and other developments strictly within psychoanalysis itself, all of which was abetted by feminist revolt against patriarchal ideology as well as by a mounting post–Vietnam War disillusionment with authority and official proclamations.

Freud's rhetorical power had less lasting effect on his analytic patients (except analytic candidates) than on the immediate and subsequent generations of readers examining his case histories. Several of the many reasons for that phenomenon merit discussion. For one, Freud's case histories possess a dazzling complexity in the nature and scope of their material. In ranging from the conscious and preconscious to the unconscious realms, Freud mixes theoretical elaboration with clinical detail, detail that he

3. Balint's historical interpretation is taken up by Haynal (1988, 33, 128).
4. See Sutherland (1980, 342).

refers to and supplements with further facts and reflections. Readers are overwhelmed by the accumulating wealth of analysis and synthesis, the whirl of detail, the leaps of imagination, and the firm self-conviction—all presented in multiple interdisciplinary perspectives and subject to constant modifications, however slight. Compared with other case writers, Freud offers astoundingly more clinical and theoretical units of thought.

Freud's unfolding of his subject matter adds to its impact. Unlike the explicit about-face near the end of his essay "Observations on Transference Love" (1915, 168), his processive modifications of his opinions and contradictory statements in the Dora case appear in soft focus, obfuscated by bountiful detail. At one point, Freud even asserts that motives for illness must occur after the symptom is formed, and he glibly proceeds in the very next paragraph to say the opposite, but without referring to what he just said—an inconsistency that he did correct in a footnote added in 1923 (43). A constant temporal indexing renders Freud's forceful complexity even more dense. Although, as I have related, Freud does make egregious errors of chronology in his case histories, the hyperawareness of time that ceaselessly inflects his prose distinguishes his case histories from all others. The temporal saturation of his narratives helps to hide their implausible elements. (An effective way of analyzing Freud's complex textuality is to follow one thread at a time and see how it changes; otherwise, one tends to get lost, led by Freud as he follows out one thread, then weaves it with a few others, the threads and weave taking on commingling shades and directions.)

One of the most commanding aspects of Freud's discourse is in its reflexive self-centeredness and other-centeredness. First, as I have elaborated elsewhere (1987), he lets us share in his reflections on his own thinking and writing processes. Second, better than anyone else, Freud tells us how to read him; his detailed commentaries on psychopathology present a map of intrapsychic miscommunication. Better yet, all his works on psychopathology are simultaneously insights into misunderstanding both oneself and others: misunderstanding, or communicative misfiring, takes on various inflections in the externalized exchanges of messages that occur in the acts of speaking and hearing or writing and reading.

Throughout his text Freud inscribes the theme of reading and misreading of any subject, including psychoanalysis. Supplementary to those commentaries are the individual strategies adopted by Freud in any one text to tell his reader how to read that text. Directly or indirectly he engages in a constant commentary on the reader's resistance, so that even if one disagrees with the ideas of a particular passage, one is drawn to agree with his comments about the subversiveness of the unconscious. His unique way of creating a readerly alliance reinforces the dialogic nature of his prose and renders it eminently internalizable; the transferential trap set by Freud's prose therefore challenges the psychoanalytic and nonpsychoanalytic reader alike. In the Dora case history and elsewhere, Freud's repeated references to friends and foes cloak his comments about competent and incompetent readers, respectively. In his self-concern Freud might also refer to the plight of another author, such as Richard von Krafft-Ebing, whose *Psychopathia Sexualis* was savaged by many who had not even read the book (50).

Much as there is a discursive specificity to a patient's free associations and an analyst's interpretations, there is a specificity to Freud's prose and an adequate interpretive response to it. All too often analysts in their reductionistic approaches to Freud's discourse tend to dismiss certain of its aspects as merely aesthetic. Relieved by such a devaluatory procedure, they believe that they can then deal with the essential scientific core of his discourse. A devaluation of that sort, though yielding the immediate satisfactions of mastery and comfort, reveals a reading-out.

Any reader is rewarded who heeds the suggestive richness of Freud's theoretical insistence about being able only to approximate the unconscious; his fluid conception of psychoanalytic language; the dialogic nature of his expressivity; and his metacommentary on reading and supple presentations of himself and the reader. The integral nature of Freud's message must not be

separated from the subplot hidden in his language, the complexity
of which is intensified by his subversion of the difference between
language and metalanguage.

Freud crafted a prose that generated as well as facilitated both
his associative and his critical processes. In order not to lose a
critical freedom, we readers of Freud must engage our associative
and critical processes. We must carry a psychoanalytically informed reading and thus analyze our own transferential reactions; and we must examine the tension between Freud's overall
counsels on how to read him and the particular tactics adopted in
any one text, especially the case histories. Such a critical itinerary
will benefit the reader who sets out to ply the troubled waters of
the Dora case.

References

Adatto, C. (1958). Ego integration observed in analyses of late adolescence. *Int. J. Psychoanal.*, 39:172–177.

——. (1966). On the metamorphosis from adolescence into adulthood. *J. Amer. Psychoanal. Assn.*, 14:484–509.

Anzieu, D. (1959, rev. ed. 1975). *L'auto-analyse de Freud et la découverte de la psychanalyse.* 2 vols. Paris: Presses Universitaires de France.

Appelby, R. 1993. Dracula and Dora: The diagnosis and treatment of alternative narratives. *Novel: The Form of Literature*, 39:16–37.

Auerbach, N. (1982). *Woman and the demon: The life of a Victorian myth.* Cambridge: Harvard University Press.

Banks, C. (1991). A dream of incest taboo, exchange of women and seduction: A reinterpretation of Freud's Dora. *Psychoanal. and Contemporary Thought*, 14:251–269.

Baum, E. (1981). Some thoughts about the Dora case: Discussion of "Transference in the Dora case" by Hyman Muslin and Merton Gill. *J. Philadelphia Assn. of Psychoanal.*, 8:25–32.

Begel, D. (1982). Three examples of countertransference in Freud's Dora case. *Amer. J. Psychoanal.*, 42:163–169.

Bernheimer, C. (1985). Introduction: Part l. In Bernheimer and Kahane, 1985, Bernheimer 1–18.

Bernheimer, C., and Kahane, C., eds. (1985). *In Dora's case: Freud-hysteria-feminism.* New York: Columbia University Press.

Bernstein, I. (1980). Integrative summary: On the re-viewing of the Dora case. In *Freud and his patients,* ed. M. Kanzer and J. Glenn, pp. 83–94. New York: Jason Aronson.

Bird, B. (1972). Notes on transference: Universal phenomenon and hardest part of analysis. *J. Amer. Psychoanal. Assn.*, 20:267–301.

Blass, R. (1992). Did Dora have an Oedipus complex? A reexamination of the theoretical content of Freud's "Fragment of an analysis." *Psychoanal. Study Child*, 47:159–187.

Blos, P. (1972). The epigenesis of an adult neurosis. *Psychoanal. Study Child*, 27:106–135.

―――. (1979). Modifications in the classical psychoanalytic model of adolescence. In *Adolescent Psychiatry*, ed. S. Sherman and P. Giovacchini, pp. 6–25. Chicago: Chicago University Press.

Blum, H. 1994. Dora's conversion syndrome: A contribution to the prehistory of the holocaust. *Psychoanal. Q.*, 53:518–535.

Brodsky, A., and Hare-Mustin, R. (1980). *Women and psychotherapy*. New York: Guilford Press.

Bornemann, E. (1984). *Sex im Volksmund*. Herrsching, Ger.: Pawlak Verlagsgesellschaft.

Buckley, P. 1989. Fifty years after Freud: Dora, the Rat Man and the Wolf Man. *Amer. J. Psychiatry*, 146:1394–1403.

Calogeras, R., and Schupper, F. (1972). Origins and early formation of the Oedipus complex. *J. Amer. Psychoanal. Assn.*, 20:751–775.

Chehrazi, S. (1986). Female psychology: A female review. *J. Amer. Psychoanal. Assn.*, 34:141–162.

Cixous, H. (1983). Portrait of Dora. *Diacritics*, 13:2–36.

Cixous, H., and Clément, C. (1975). *La jeune née*. Paris: Union Générale d'Editions.

Cohn, D. (1992). Freud's case histories and the question of fictionality. In *Telling facts: History and narration in psychoanalysis*, ed. J. Smith and H. Morris, pp. 21–47. Baltimore: Johns Hopkins University Press.

Collins, D., et al. (1983). Questioning the unconscious: The Dora archives. *Diacritics*, 13:37–42.

Cornut, J. (1974). Construction, résistance et transfert (un commentaire de "Dora"). *Europe: Revue littéraire mensuel*, 539:15–31.

Crapanzano, V. (1981). Text, transference, and indexicality. *Ethos*, 9:122–148.

David, C. (1974). Discussion of paper by René Major on "The revolution of hysteria." *Int. J. Psychoanal.*, 55:393–395.

David-Ménard, M. (1989). *Hysteria from Freud to Lacan*. Ithaca, N.Y.: Cornell University Press.

Davis, R. (1993). *Freud's concept of passivity*. Madison, Conn.: International Universities Press.

Decker, H. (1981). Freud and Dora: Constraints on medical progress. *J. Soc. Hist.*, 14:445–464.

——. (1982). The choice of a name: "Dora" and Freud's relationship with Breuer. *J. Amer. Psychoanal. Assn.*, 30:87–111.

——. (1991). *Freud, Dora, and Vienna, 1900*. New York: Free Press.

Deutsch, F. (1957). A footnote to Freud's analysis of an "Analysis of a case of hysteria." *Psychoanal. Q.*, 62:159–167.

Didi-Huberman, G. (1982). *Invention de l'hystérie*. Paris: Macula.

Eissler, K. (1972). *Talent and genius*. New York: Quadrangle Books.

——. (1986). *Freud as an expert witness: The discussion of war neuroses between Freud and Wagner-Jauregg*. Madison, Conn.: International Universities Press.

Erlich, I. (1977). What happened to Jocasta? *Bull. Menninger Clinic*, 41:280–284.

Erikson, E. (1964). *Insight and responsibility*. New York: Norton.

——. (1968). *Identity: Youth and crisis*. New York: Norton.

Eysenck, H. (1965). *Decline and fall of the Freudian empire*. New York: Viking.

Firestein, S. (1982). Termination of psychoanalysis: Theoretical, clinical, and pedagogic considerations. *Psychoanal. Inquiry*, 2:473–497.

Forrester, J., and Appignanesi, L. (1992). *Freud's women*. New York: Basic Books.

Fraiberg, S. (1955). Some considerations on the introduction to therapy in puberty. *Psychoanal. Study Child*, 10:264–286.

Frank, L. (1989). Freud and Dora: Blindness and insight. In *Seduction and theory*. Ed. D. Hunter, pp. 110–134. Urbana: University of Illinois Press.

French, T. (1954). *The integration of behavior*, vol. 2: *The integrative process in dreams*. Chicago: Chicago University Press.

Freud, S. (1940–1952). *Gesammelte Werke*. 17 vols. Frankfurt am Main: S. Fischer. Abbreviated as *G.W.*

——. (1953–1974). *The standard edition of the complete psychological works*. Ed. and trans. J. Strachey. 24 vols. London: Hogarth. Abbreviated as *S.E.*

——. (1893–1895). *Studies on hysteria*. In *S.E.*, 2.

——. (1896a). The aetiology of hysteria. In *S.E.*, 3:187–221.

———. (1896b). Further remarks on the neuro-psychoses of defence. In *S.E.*, 3:159–188. Also in *G.W.*, 1:379–403.

———. (1898). Sexuality in the theory of neuroses. In *S.E.*, 3:261–286.

———. (1899). Screen memories. In *S.E.*, 3:301–322.

———. (1900). *The interpretation of dreams.* In *S.E.*, 4–5.

———. (1901). *The psychopathology of everyday life.* In *S.E.*, 6.

———. (1905a). Fragment of an analysis of a case of hysteria. In *S.E.*, 7:3–122.

———. (1905b). *Three essays on the theory of sexuality.* In *S.E.*, 7:222–243.

———. (1909). Notes upon a case of obsessional neurosis. In *S.E.*, 10:153–318.

———. (1910). Leonardo da Vinci and a memory of his childhood. In *S.E.*, 11:59–137.

———. (1912). Recommendations to physicians practicing psychoanalysis. In *S.E.*, 12:109–120.

———. (1913a). On beginning the treatment. In *S.E.*, 12:121–144.

———. (1913b). The theme of the three caskets. In *S.E.*, 12:289–302.

———. (1913c). Totem and taboo. In *S.E.*, 13:1–162.

———. (1914). On the history of the psychoanalytic movement. In *S.E.*, 14:3–66.

———. (1915). Observations on transference-love. In *S.E.*, 12:157–161.

———. (1915–1916). *Introductory lectures on psychoanalysis.* In *S.E.*, 15.

———. (1918). From the history of an infantile neurosis. In *S.E.*, 17:3–122. Also in *G.W.*, 12:29–157.

———. (1920). Beyond the pleasure principle. In *S.E.*, 18:7–64.

———. (1921). Group psychology and the analysis of the ego. In *S.E.*, 18:67–144.

———. (1925). Some psychical consequences of the anatomical distinction between the sexes. In *S.E.*, 19:243–258.

———. (1926). Inhibitions, symptoms and anxiety. In *S.E.*, 20:77–178.

———. (1930). Civilization and its discontents. In *S.E.*, 21:59–145.

———. (1937). Analysis terminable and interminable. In *S.E.*, 23:211–253.

———. (1939). Moses and monotheism. In *S.E.*, 23:3–138.

———. (1960). *Letters of Sigmund Freud (1873–1939).* Ed. E. Freud. London: Hogarth Press.

————. (1965). *A psychoanalytic dialogue: The letters of Sigmund Freud and Karl Abraham, 1907–1926.* Eds. H. Abraham and E. Freud. London: Hogarth Press.

————. (1974). *The Freud/Jung letters.* Ed. J. W. McGuire. Princeton: Princeton University Press.

————. (1985). *The complete letters of Sigmund Freud to Wilhelm Fliess (1877–1904).* Ed. and trans. J. Masson. Cambridge: Harvard University Press. Also published in a German edition: Freud, 1986.

————. (1986). *Sigmund Freud: Briefe an Wilhelm Fliess, 1887–1904.* Ed. J. Masson. Frankfurt am Main: S. Fischer.

————. (1993a). *The complete correspondence of Sigmund Freud and Ernest Jones, 1908–1939.* Ed. R. Paskauskas. Cambridge: Harvard University Press.

————. (1993b). *The correspondence of Sigmund Freud and Sandor Ferenczi, 1908–1914.* Ed. E. Brabant, E. Falzeder, and P. Giapieri-Deutsch. Vol. l. Cambridge: Harvard University Press.

Gallop, J. (1982). *The daughter's seduction: Feminism and psychoanalysis.* Ithaca, N.Y.: Cornell University Press.

Gay, P. (1988). *Freud: A life for our time.* New York: Norton.

Geahchan, D. (1973). Haine et identification négative dans l'hystérie. *Revue française de psychanalyse,* 37:337–358.

Gearhart, S. (1979). The scene of psychoanalysis: The unanswered questions of Dora. *Diacritics,* 9:114–126.

Gilman, S. (1991). *The Jew's body.* New York: Routledge.

————. (1993). The image of the hysteric. In *Hysteria beyond Freud,* ed. S. Gilman, pp. 345–452. Berkeley: University of California Press.

Glenn, J. (1980a). Freud's adolescent patients: Katharina, Dora and the "Homosexual Woman." In *Freud and his patients,* ed. M. Kanzer and J. Glenn, pp. 23–47. New York: Jason Aronson.

————. (1980b). Notes on psychoanalytic concepts and style in Freud's case histories. In *Freud and his patients,* ed. M. Kanzer and J. Glenn, pp. 3–22. New York: Jason Aronson.

————. (1986). Freud, Dora, and the maid: A study of countertransference. *J. Amer. Psychoanal. Assn.,* 34:591–635.

————. (1993). Dora's dynamics, diagnosis, and treatment: Old and modern views. *Annual of Psychoanal.,* 21:125–138.

Gordon, R. (1984). Desire in woman: A Jungian approach. In *ICA Documents: Desire,* pp. 14–16. London: Institute of Contemporary Arts.

Hare-Mustin, R. (1983). An appraisal of the relationship between women in psychotherapy: Eighty years after the case of Dora. *Amer. Psychol.*, 38:593–610.

Hertz, N. (1983). Dora's secrets, Freud's techniques. *Diacritics*, 13:65–76.

Hollande, C. (1993). A propos de l'identification hystérique. *Revue française de psychanalyse*, 37:323–330.

Irigaray, L. (1974). *Spéculum de l'autre femme*. Paris: Minuit.

Jacobus, M. (1986). *Reading woman: Essays in feminist criticism*. New York: Columbia University Press.

Jennings, J. (1986). The revival of "Dora": Advances in psychoanalytic theory and technique. *J. Amer. Psychoanal. Assn.*, 34:607–636.

Jones, E. (1953 and 1955). *The life and work of Sigmund Freud*. 2 vols. New York: Basic Books.

Josefine Mutzenbacher (1904 or 1906, new ed. 1978). Hamburg: Reinbek.

Kafka, E. (1994). Book review of H. Decker, *Freud, Dora, and Vienna, 1900*. *J. Amer. Psychoanal. Assn.*, 42:894–898.

Kahane, C. (1985). Introduction: Part 2. In Bernheimer and Kahane, 1985, 19–32.

Kanzer, M. (1980). Dora's imagery: The flight from a burning house. In *Freud and his patients*, ed. M. Kanzer and J. Glenn, pp. 58–71. New York: Jason Aronson.

Katz, S. (1987). Speaking out against the "talking cure": Unmarried women in Freud's early case studies. *Women's Studies*, 13:297–324.

Kemple, T. (1989). Dora from A to Z: A fragmentary misreading. *Discours social: Social Discourse*, 2:37–44.

Keill, N., ed. (1988). *Freud without hindsight: Reviews of his work, 1893–1939*. Madison, Conn.: International Universities Press.

Kofman, S. (1980). *L'énigme de la femme*. Paris: Galilée.

Kohon, G. (1983). Reflections on Dora: The case of hysteria. *Int. J. Psychoanal.*, 65:73–84.

Krohn, A., and Krohn J. (1982). The nature of the Oedipus complex in the Dora case. *J. Amer. Psychoanal. Assn.*, 30:555–578.

Lacan, J. (1951). Intervention sur le transfert. In Lacan, *Ecrits*, pp. 215–226. Paris: Seuil, 1966.

———. (1954). Les fluctuations de la libido. In Lacan, *Le séminaire III: Les écrits techniques de Freud*, pp. 199–210. Paris: Seuil, 1975.

———. (1956). La question hystérique (II): "Qu'est-ce qu'une femme?" In Lacan, *Le séminaire III: Les psychoses*. Paris: Seuil, 1981.

―――. (1964). Du sujet de la certitude: Les quatres concepts fondamentaux de la psychanalyse. In Lacan, *Les quatres concepts fondamentaux de la psychanalyse*, pp. 31–41. Paris: Seuil, 1973.

Langs, R. (1976). The misalliance dimension in Freud's case histories: I. The case of Dora. *Int. J. Psychoanal. Psychotherapy*, 5:301–318.

Laplanche, J., and Pontalis, J.-B. (1978). *Vocabulaire de la psychanalyse.* Paris: Presses Universitaires de France.

Laurent, E. (1986). Lectures de Dora. In Laurent, *Hystérie et obsession*, pp. 29–42. Paris: Fondation du Champs Freudien.

Lewis, K. (1973). Dora revisited. *Psychoanal. Rev.*, 60:519–532.

Le Rider, J. (1982). *Le cas Otto Weininger.* Paris: Presses Universitaires de France.

Loewenberg, P. (1983). *Decoding the past: The psychohistorical approach.* New York: Knopf.

Loewenstein, E. (1992). The Freudian case history: A detective story or a dialectical progression? Reflection on psychoanalytic narratives from a Lacanian perspective. *Psychoanal. Psychol.*, 9:49–59.

―――. (1993). The limitation of a positivistic approach to psychoanalytic history: A reply to Naso's commentary. *Psychoanal. Psychol.*, 10: 105–11.

―――. (1994). Dissolving the myth of the unified self: The fate of the subject in Freudian analysis. *Psychoanal. Q.*, 53:715–732.

Lopez, D. (1990). Frau K and Dora. In *Criticism and Lacan: Essays and dialogue on language, structure, and the unconscious*, ed. P. Hogan and L. Pandit, pp. 180–184. Athens: University of Georgia Press.

Lubtchansky, J. (1973). Le point de vue économique dans l'hystérie à partir de la notion du traumatisme dans l'oeuvre de Freud. *Revue française de psychanalyse*, 37:373–406.

Macmillan, M. (1991). *Freud evaluated: The completed arc.* Amsterdam: North-Holland.

Mahony, P. (1979). Friendship and its discontents. *Contemporary Psychoanal.*, 15:55–109.

―――. (1984). *Cries of the Wolf Man.* New York: International Universities Press. Also published in a thoroughly revised French edition: Mahony, 1995.

―――. (1986a). *Freud and the Rat Man.* New Haven: Yale University Press. Also published in a French translation: Mahony, 1991.

―――. (1986b). *Psychoanalysis and discourse.* London: Tavistock and Routledge.

————. (1987, rev. ed.). *Freud as a writer*. New Haven: Yale University Press.

————. (1989). *On defining Freud's discourse*. New Haven: Yale University Press.

————. (1991). *Freud et l'homme aux rats*. Trans. Bertrand Vichyn. Paris: Presses Universitaires de France.

————. (1993a). Freud's cases: Are they valuable today? *Int. J. Psychoanal.*, 74:1027–1035.

————. (1993b). The dictator and his cure. *Int. J. Psychoanal.*, 74:1245–1251.

————. (1994). Psychoanalysis—The writing cure. In *One Hundred Years of Psychoanalysis*, ed. A. Haynal and E. Falzeder. Geneva: Cahiers Psychiatriques Genevois et Institutions Universitaires de Psychiatrie de Genève.

————. (1995). *Les hurlements de l'homme aux loups*. Trans. Bertrand Vichyn. Paris: Presses Universitaires de France.

Major, R. (1974). The revolution of hysteria. *Int. J. Psychoanal.*, 55:385–395.

Malcolm, J. (1981). *Psychoanalysis: The impossible profession*. New York: Knopf.

————. (1987). Reflections: J'appelle un chat un chat. *New Yorker*, April 21, pp. 84–102.

Marcus, J. (1976). Freud and Dora: Story, history, case history. *Psychoanal. and Contemporary Thought*, 5:389–442.

Marty, P., et al. (1968). Le cas Dora et le point de vue psychosomatique. *Revue française de psychanalyse*, 32:679–714.

Masson, J. (1988). *Against therapy*. New York: Atheneum.

McCaffrey, P. (1984). *Freud and Dora: The artful dream*. New Brunswick, N.J.: Rutgers University Press.

Meissner, W. (1984–1985). Studies on hysteria: Dora. *Int. J. Psychoanal. and Psychotherapy*, 10:567–598.

Mijolla, A., de. (1989). Images de Freud, au travers de sa correspondence. *Rev. Int. Hist. Psychanal.*, 2:9–50.

Mitchell, J. (1983). Introduction: l. In *Feminine sexuality: Jacques Lacan and the école freudiennne*, ed. J. Mitchell and J. Rose, pp. 1–26. New York: Pantheon.

Moi, Toril. (1985). Representation of patriarchy: Sexuality and epistemology in Freud's Dora. In Bernheimer and Kahane, 1985, 181–199.

————. (1984). Psychoanalysis and desire: The case of Dora. *ICA Documents: Desire*, p. 3. London: Institute of Contemporary Arts.

Morris, H. (1992). Translating transmission: Representation and enactment in Freud's construction of history. In *Telling facts: History and narration in psychoanalysis*, ed. J. Smith and H. Morris, pp. 48–102. Baltimore: Johns Hopkins University Press.

Moscovitz, J. (1973). D'un signe qui lui serait fait, ou aspects de l'homosexualité dans "Dora." *Revue française de psychanalyse*, 37:359–372.

Muslin, H., and Gill, M. (1978). Transference in the Dora case. *J. Amer. Psychoanal. Assn.*, 26:311–330.

Nelson Garner, S., Kahane, C., and Sprengnether, M., eds. (1985). *The m/other tongue: Essays in feminist psychoanalytic interpretation.* Ithaca, N.Y.: Cornell University Press.

Nietzsche, Friedrich. (1954). Preface to *Ecce Homo.* In *The Philosophy of Nietzsche*, trans. Clifton Fadiman, pp. 811–814. New York: Modern Library.

Nunberg, H., and Federn, E., eds. (1962, 1967, 1974). *Minutes of the Vienna Psychoanalytic Society.* Vols. 1–3. New York: International Universities Press.

Olsen, O., and Koppe, S. (1988). *Freud's theory of psychoanalysis.* New York: New York University Press.

Ornstein, P. (1993). Did Freud understand Dora? In *Freud's case histories: Self-psychological perspectives*, ed. B. Magid, pp. 31–86. Hillsdale, N.J.: Analytic Press.

Ornston, D., ed. (1992). *Translating Freud.* New Haven: Yale University Press.

Possick, S. (1984). Termination in the Dora case. *J. Amer. Academy Psychoanal.*, 12:1–11.

Raglund-Sullivan, E. (1989). Dora and the name-of-the-father: The structure of hysteria. In *Discontented discourses: Feminism/textual intervention/psychoanalysis*, ed. M. Barr and R. Feldstein, pp. 208–240. Urbana: University of Illinois Press.

Ramas, M. (1980). Freud's Dora, Dora's hysteria: The negation of a woman's rebellion. *Feminist Studies*, 6:472–510.

Rieff, P., ed. (1963). *Dora: An analysis of a case of hysteria.* New York: Collier.

————. (1972). *Fellow teachers.* New York: Harper and Row.

————. (1979). *Freud: The mind of a moralist.* Chicago: University of Chicago Press.

Roazen, P. (1994). Freud's Dora and Felix Deutsch. *Psychologist/Psychoanalyst*, 15:34–36.

Robins, C. (1991). Dora's dreams: In whose voice—Strachey's, Freud's or Dora's? *Contemporary Psychotherapy Review*, 6:44–79.

Rogow, A. (1978). A further footnote to Freud's "Fragment of an analysis of a case of hysteria." *J. Amer. Psychoanal. Assn.*, 26:311–330.

———. (1979). Dora's brother. *Int. Rev. Psychoanal.*, 6:239–259.

Roof, J. (1991). *A lure of knowledge*. New York: Columbia University Press.

Rose, J. (1978). Dora: Fragment of an analysis. *M/F: A feminist journal*, 2:5–21.

Sand, R. (1983). Confirmation in the Dora case. *Int. Rev. Psychoanal.*, 10:333–357.

Shafer, R. (1977). A new female psychology? In *Female psychology*, ed. H. Blum, pp. 393–438. New York: International Universities Press.

Scharfman, M. (1980). Further reflections on Dora. In *Freud and his patients*, ed. M. Kanzer and J. Glenn, pp. 48–57. New York: Jason Aronson.

Schimmel, I. (1973). Rêve et transfer dans "Dora." *Revue française de psychanalyse*, 37:313–322.

Schlesier, R. (1981). *Konstruktionen der Weiblichkeit bei Sigmund Freud*. Frankfurt am Main: Europäische Verlagamstatt.

Schorske, C. (1993). Freud's Egyptian dig. *New York Review of Books* (May 27), 41:35–40.

Schur, M. (1972). *Freud: Living and dying*. New York: International Universities Press.

Seidenberg, R., and Papathomopoulos, E. (1962). Daughters who tend their fathers. *Psychoanal. Study of Society*, 2:135–160.

Showalter, E. (1987). *The female malady: Women, madness, and English culture*. New York: Penguin.

Slipp, S. (1977). Interpersonal factors in hysteria: Freud's seduction theory and the case of Dora. *J. Amer. Acad. Psychoanal.*, 5:359–376.

Spence, D. (1986). When interpretation masquerades as explanation. *J. Amer. Psychoanal. Assn.*, 34:3–22.

———. (1987). *The Freudian metaphor*. New York: Norton.

Sprengnether, M. (1985). Enforcing Oedipus: Freud and Dora. In Bernheimer and Kahane, 1985, 254–276.

———. (1990). *The spectral mother: Freud, feminism, and psychoanalysis*. Ithaca, N.Y.: Cornell University Press.

Stadlen, A. (1989). Was Dora "ill"?. In *Sigmund Freud: Critical assessments*, ed. L. Spurling, 2:196–203. New York: Routledge.

Steiner, R. (1984). Dora: "La belle indifference" or "Label(le) in différence." *ICA Documents: Desire*, pp. 9–13. London: Institute of Contemporary Arts.

Steinberg, S. (1986). The master tropes of dreaming: Rhetoric as a family affair. *Amer. J. Semiotics*, 4:29–51.

Stroeken, H. (1987). *En analyse avec Freud*. Paris: Payot.

Sulieman, S. (1988). Mastery and transference: The significance of *Dora*. In *The comparative perspective on literature: Approaches to theory and practice*, ed. C. Koelb and S. Noakes, pp. 213–223. Ithaca, N.Y.: Cornell University Press.

Thompson, A. (1990). The ending to Dora's story: Deutsch's footnote as narrative. *Psychoanal. and Contemporary Thought*, 13:509–534.

Timms, E. (1982). Novelle and case history: Freud in pursuit of the falcon. *London German Studies*, 2:115–134.

van den Berg, S. (1986). Reading Dora reading. *Literature and Psychology*, 32:27–35.

———. (1987). Reading and writing Dora: Preoedipal conflict in Freud's "Fragment of an analysis of a case of hysteria." *Psychoanal. and Contemporary Thought*, 10:45–67.

Viderman, S. (1974). Interpretation in the analytic space. *Int. Rev. Psychoanal.*, 1:467–480.

———. (1977). *Le céleste et le sublunaire*. Paris: Presses Universitaires de France.

Ville, E. (1973). Analité et hystérie. *Revue française de psychanalyse*, 37: 331–336.

Weiss, E. (1970). *Sigmund Freud as a consultant*. New York: Intercontinental Medical Book Corporation.

Willis, S. (1983). A symptomatic narrative. *Diacritics*, 13:46–64.

Wolstein, B. (1954). *Transference: Its meaning and formation in psychoanalytic therapy*. New York: Grune and Stratton.

Index

Abraham, Karl, 62, 147*n*
Achensee, 22, 25
"Aetiology of Hysteria, The," 59
"Analysis Terminable and Interminable," 23

B——. *See* Merano
Bauer, Ida. *See* Dora
Bauer, Kätharina (Käthe) (Dora's mother): character, 2–4, 53, 79, 87–88, 102; complicity in her husband's liaison, 12; biographical data, 17–20, 101; ignored by Freud, 44; Dora's reactions to, 44, 70–72, 80
Bauer, Otto (Dora's brother): 3–5, 8, 15–17, 21, 40, 71, 74, 79, 134–135
Bauer, Philip (Dora's father): illness, 3, 7–8, 53, 72, 75, 144; character, 3–4; liaison with Peppina Zellenka, 8–9, 12; attitude toward Dora's therapy with Freud, 13, 19–20, 34, 44, 79, 143; biographical data, 17–21
Beer-Hofmann, Richard, 48
"Beyond the Pleasure Principle," 48
Bonaparte, Marie, 23
Breslau, 23, 25
Breuer, Josef, 48, 126, 142
Brodmann, Korbinian, 141

case history: compared with vignette, ix, xii; difficult to read and write, ix–x; writer's empathy with reader, x–xi. *See also* Dora's case history; Freud's writing; *and specific case histories by name*
Charcot, Jean, 35*n*
"Civilization and Its Discontents," 55

Decker, Hannah, xiv, 6*n*, 17*n*, 18*n*, 19*n*, 20*n*, 36*n*, 40*n*
Deutsch, Felix, 15–16, 21, 44, 60, 63, 71, 99*n*
Didi-Huberman, Georges, 34*n*
Dora (Ida Bauer): victim of abuse, xiii, 2, 8–16, 18, 34–42, 53–74, 143–144, 146–148; etymology of the name Dora, 2; her symptoms, 5–9, 13–20, 27–30, 34, 36, 40–41, 52–76, 98–99; slippage in developmental designations, 9, 52, 97, 144; favorite aunt (Malvine), 12, 17, 18, 19, 34, 99; her governess, 12, 20, 38*n*, 40, 42, 59*n*, 60, 69, 71; source of her knowledge, 12, 30*n*, 37–39; husband, 14, 20, 21; son, 14, 20; identifications, 27, 28, 44, 59*n*, 69–73, 99*n*, 144–145; bisexuality, 27–28, 70–72; adolescent development, 34, 39, 57, 70*n*, 72–75; diagnosis, 69–75